Loie Hollowell

Space Between, A Survey of Ten Years

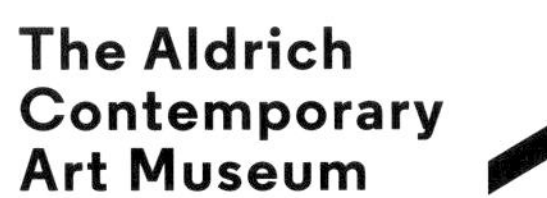

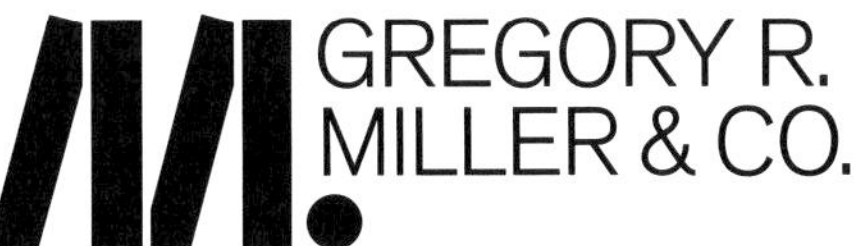

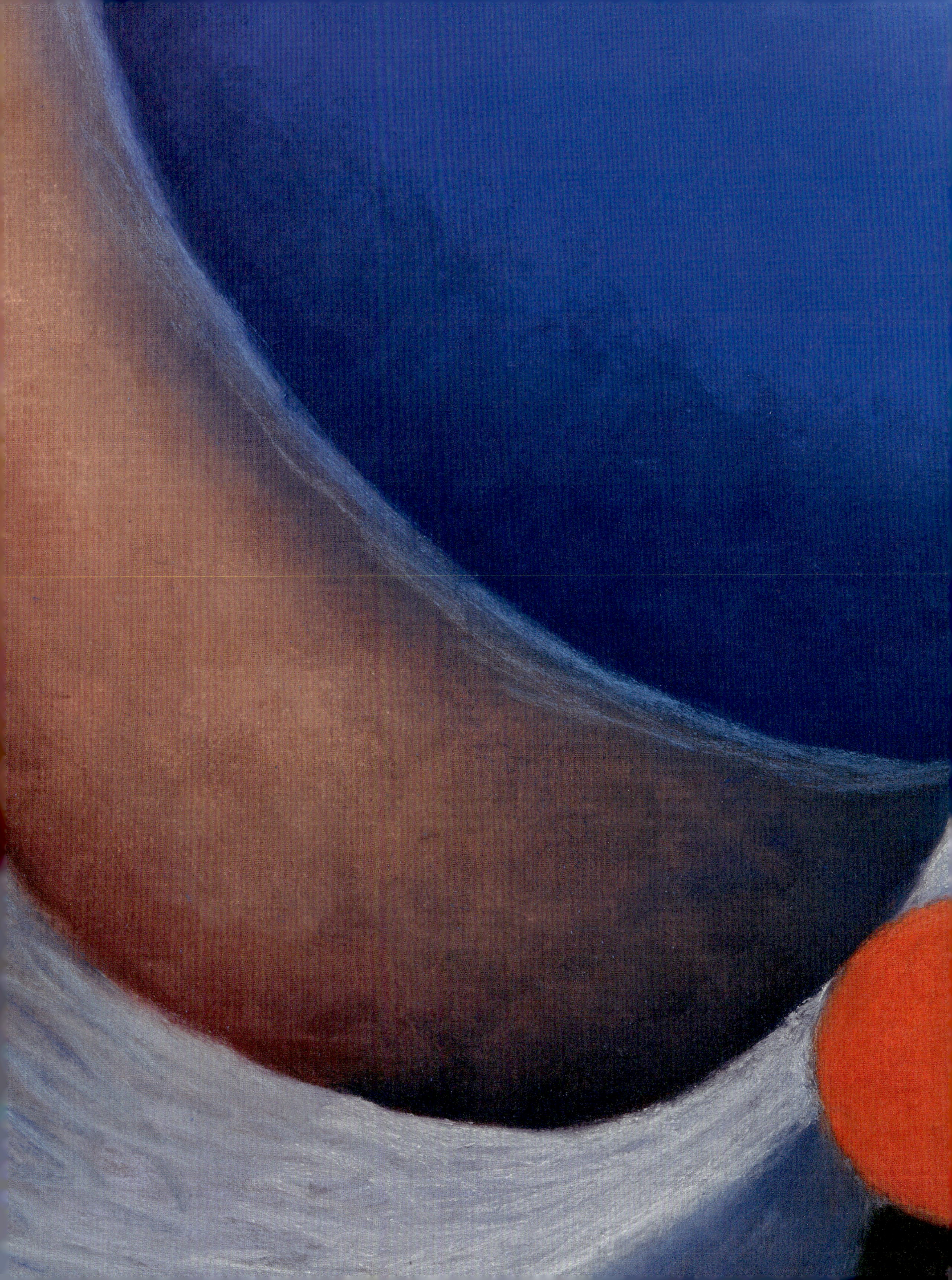

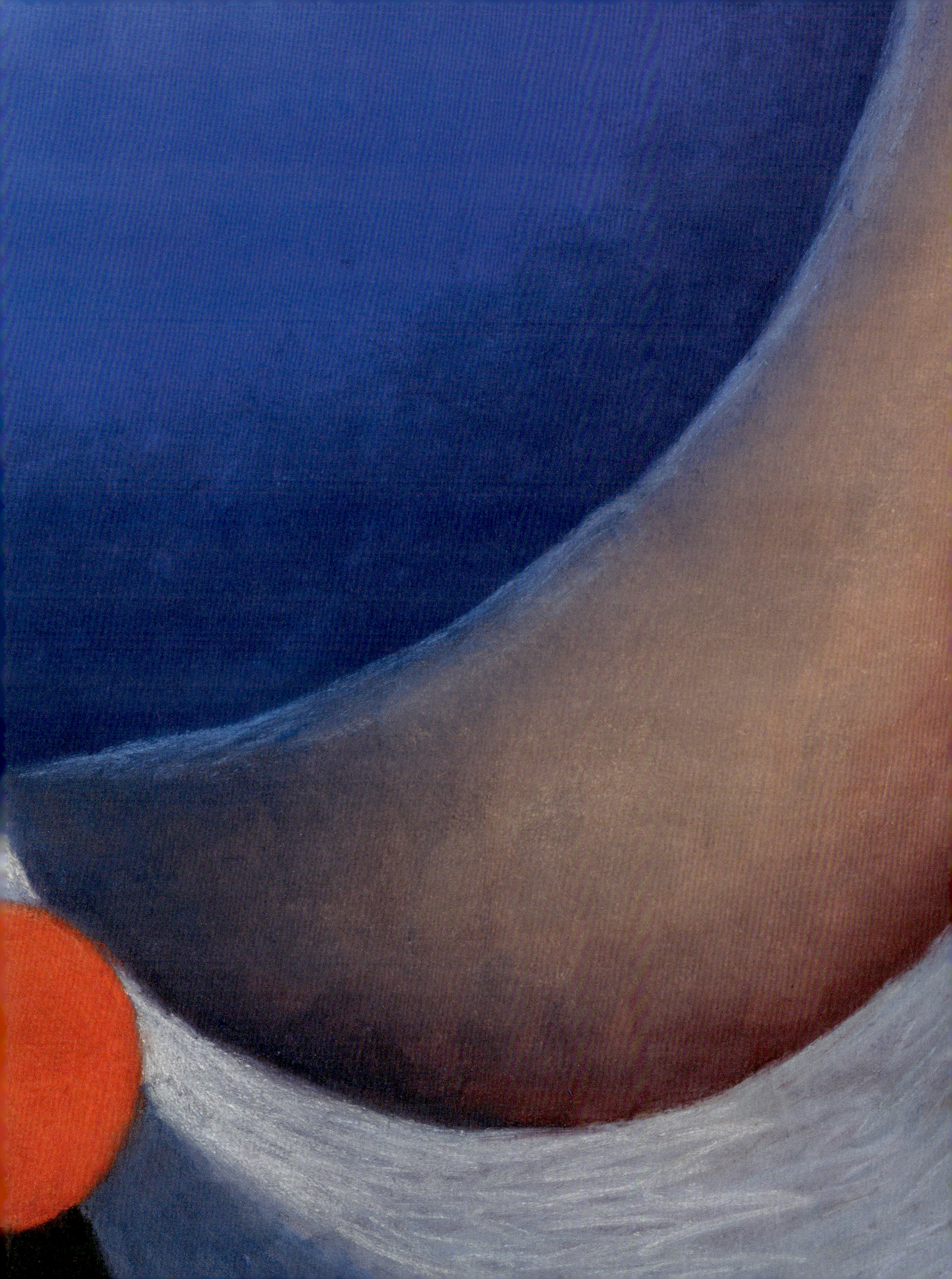

Contents

Foreword

by Cybele Maylone

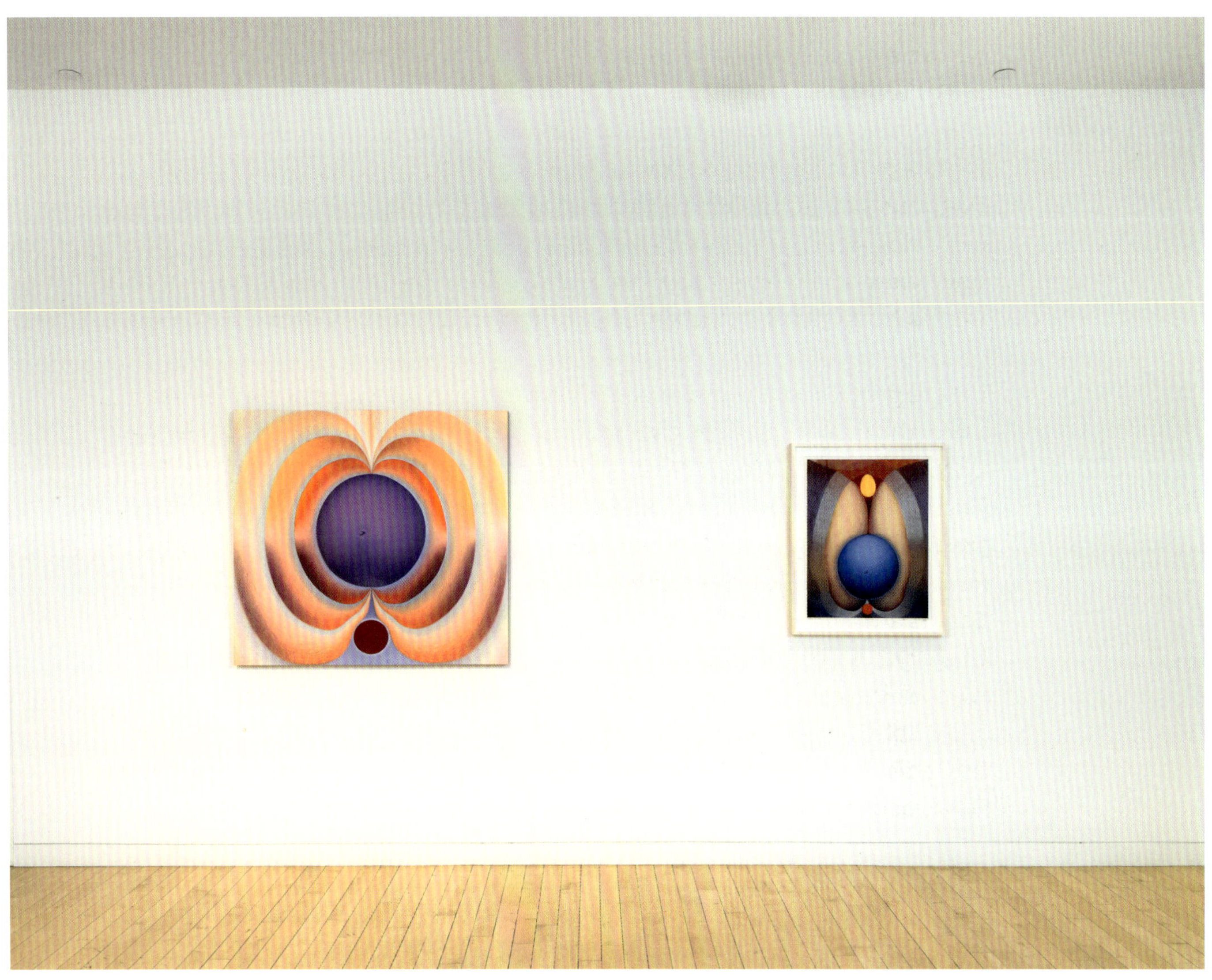

Loie Hollowell: Space Between, A Survey of Ten Years (installation view), The Aldrich Contemporary Art Museum, January 21 to August 11, 2024.

In 2019 Chief Curator Amy Smith-Stewart came to my office breathlessly sharing her enthusiasm for the work of Loie Hollowell. Amy made me promise to go see the work in person, knowing that the images on my computer screen wouldn't do the paintings justice. This was the beginning of an important relationship between Loie and The Aldrich.

Three years later, in 2022, the Museum presented *52 Artists: A Feminist Milestone*, revisiting Lucy R. Lippard's seminal 1971 exhibition for The Aldrich, *Twenty Six Contemporary Women Artists. 52 Artists* didn't simply restage Lippard's show, but rather expanded it to include a younger group of trailblazing female and nonbinary artists, tracking five decades of feminist artistic practice. Loie's painting *Empty Belly*, 2022, hung in the Museum's Leir Atrium, greeting visitors and setting the stage. While organizing *52 Artists*, Amy spent hours with Loie in the studio, and it became clear that the time was right for a more significant exploration of her work.

We are proud to present *Space Between, A Survey of Ten Years*, Loie's first museum exhibition on the East Coast and her first museum survey. Featuring new and never-before-seen work, along with paintings borrowed from numerous private collections, the exhibition tracks Loie's moves between abstraction and figuration, and painting and sculpture.

We are grateful to the many generous donors whose support helped to make this ambitious exhibition and publication possible, including Fairfax Dorn and Marc Glimcher, Jessica Silverman, Georganne Aldrich Heller, Tammy and Jay Levine, and James Park. The catalogue was supported by the Eric Diefenbach and James-Keith Brown Publications Fund, Girlfriend Fund, and Pace Gallery; production support was provided by the Diana Bowes and Jim Torrey Commissions Fund. We are fortunate to work with Gregory R. Miller & Co. as a co-publisher, and we thank Greg and his team for their insights and support. The book was designed by The Aldrich's incredible Design Director, Gretchen Kraus, and shepherded to completion by Caitlin Monachino, Curatorial and Publications Manager, and Emily Devoe, Director of Marketing and Communications.

Amy's enthusiasm for Loie's work has only grown, and I am appreciative of her vision in bringing *Space Between, A Survey of Ten Years* to life. And we are, of course, most grateful to Loie for sharing her world with The Aldrich.

Hard and Soft: The Sentient and Sensual Abstractions of Loie Hollowell

by Amy Smith-Stewart

Mother I am
Identical
With infinite Maternity
  Indivisible
  Acutely
  I am absorbed
  Into
The was—is—ever—shall—be
Of cosmic reproductivity
- Mina Loy[1]

My work is a confessional.
- Louise Bourgeois[2]

The body is a clock. This is most prominently perceived during pregnancy and its immediate aftermath, as dramatic shifts, visible and internalized, alter figure and mind, stretching it to the extremes. Loie Hollowell exploits her own body as material and content to document intervals of time and change, its elasticity and blunt force, expressed through arresting chiaroscuro, effulgent color, and charged light. She employs a visual glossary of recurring biomorphic and geometric shapes that represent human anatomy, symbols and elements lifted from spiritual and architectural sources instrumentalized for her own devices—ogees[3] for breasts, a mandorla[4] for the vulva, and the lingam[5] for the phallus—as well as life-size casts of her own and others' pregnant bellies and breasts. Her methodology is laborious, beginning with sketches that are then translated into pastel drawings later made into paintings, with compositions that are built up and textured to manifest curves, bumps, and swellings. Her palettes and configurations distill her mental and physical transitions from conception, pregnancy, and birth to postpartum after bearing two children. In her sentient and sensual abstractions, color and light are both hard and soft.

By evading the boundaries between figuration and abstraction as well as the private and radical, Hollowell makes work that operates in the distance between binary thresholds: turning hard edges supple, making light and shadow tangible, and imbuing colors with deep feeling. Her palette glows, vibrates, and blazes with luminescent progressions of reds, blues, yellows, oranges, greens, pinks, and purples that flaunt a mercurial aura from tender to explosive. Applying a rigorous symmetry in reference to the material body, she choreographs the vitality and fervency that come from the perceptual and corporeal with an emphasis she discloses on the "birthing body":[6] the epicenter of the universe, where the lower and higher realms intersect.

Space Between surveys the artist's output over ten years, paintings and works on paper at varying scales and tempos, tracking the development of a visual language that bridges autobiography and art history, biology and emotion, and Eastern and Western imagery. The exhibition's focus contemplates time as substance, allegory, and theme as Hollowell often includes signs and registers of time's process and passage within her configurations: scales, pendulums, apertures, wheels, and cycles—markers of time's speed and sweep.

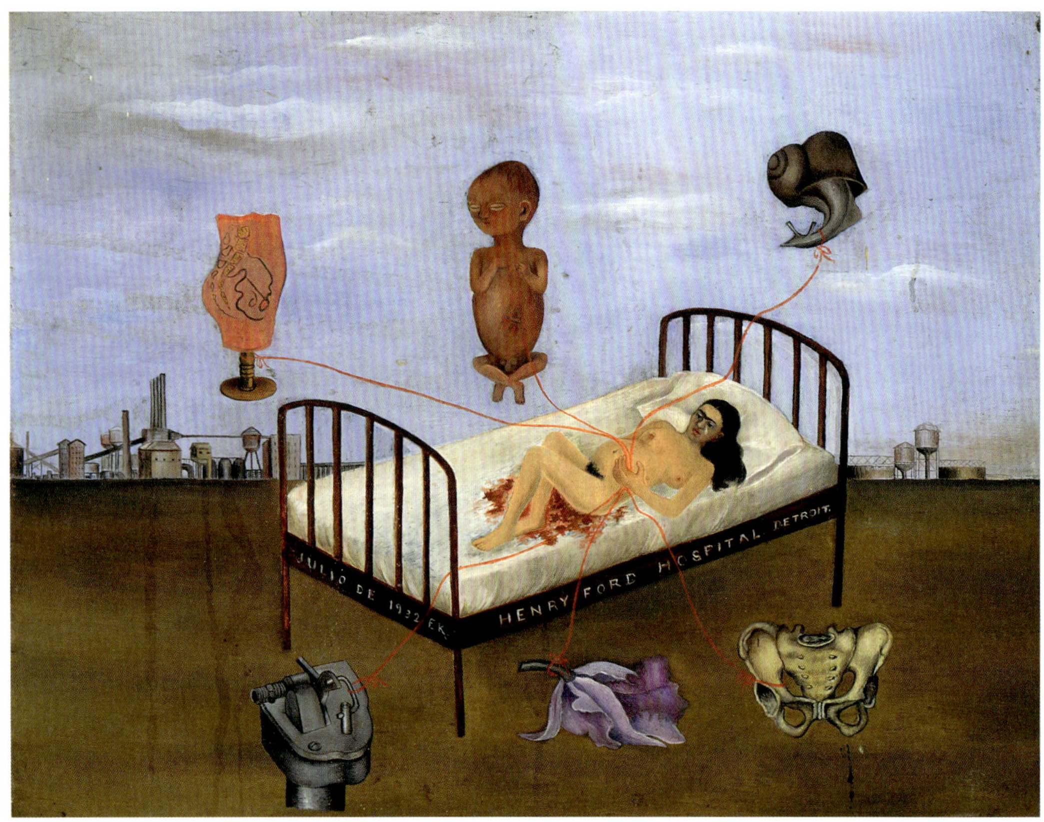

FIG. 1

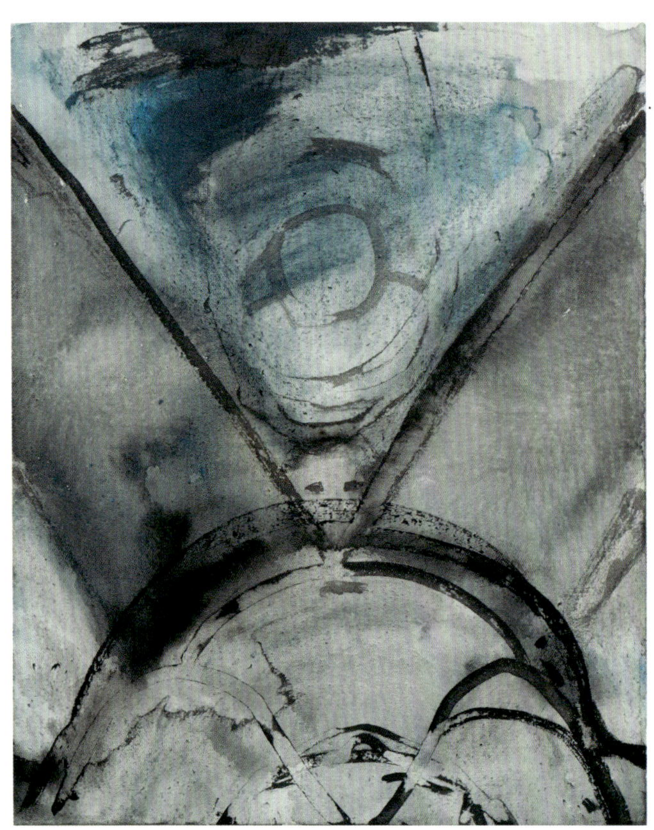

FIG. 4

1. Frida Kahlo
   Henry Ford Hospital, 1932

2. Louise Bourgeois
   UNTITLED (WOMAN GIVING BIRTH), 1941

3. Clarity Haynes
   Blood Altar, 2023

4. Luchita Hurtado
   Untitled (Birthing Mother Earth), 2018

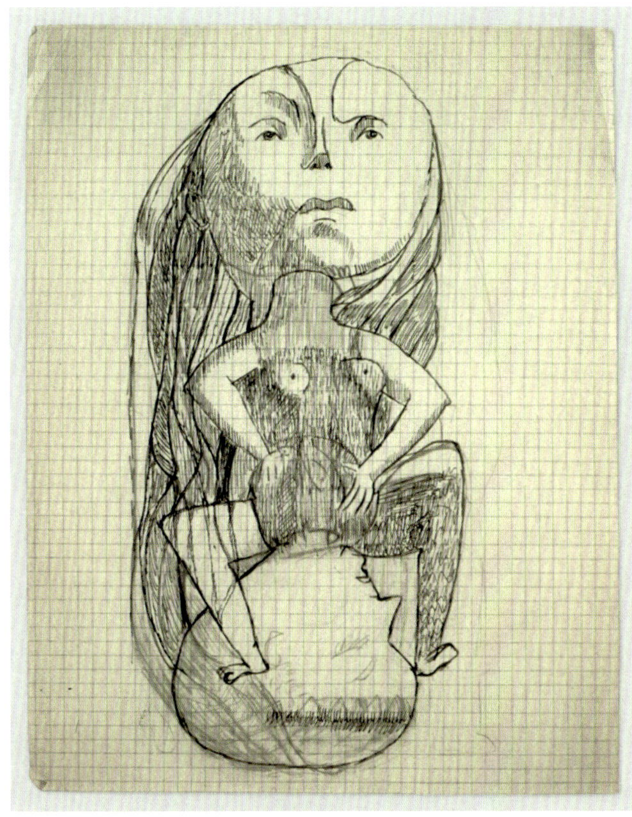

FIG. 2

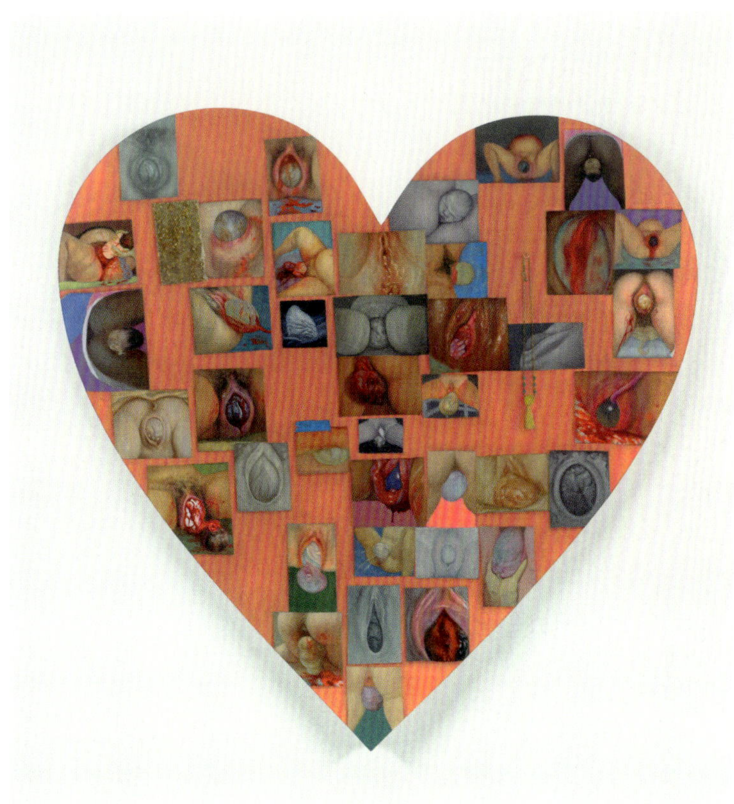

FIG. 3

She transforms the female figure into a metaphorical hourglass, integrating pigmented gradients to indicate and amplify sequential motion and acute sensation, from sexual intercourse to the dilation and contractions during parturition and the "letting down" of lactating breasts.

A self-proclaimed feminist, Hollowell cites pioneering women artists who span generations and movements over two centuries, from mystics, transcendentalists, and modernists to surrealists, feminists, and minimalists: Hilma af Klint, Agnes Pelton, Ithell Colquhoun, Georgia O'Keeffe, Louise Bourgeois, Judy Chicago, Evelyn Statsinger, and Helen Pashgian, to name just a few. But she also identifies Neo-Tantric artists such as Biren De and G. R. Santosh as important influences.[7] She uses the innermost circumstances of her own body to counter a historically hetero-patriarchal canon, asserting matter and experiences absent in art history and culture at large to appraise seismic social issues, from sexual liberation to feminism, from reproductive rights to motherhood, while also celebrating the potency and magnificence of matriarchy. Although the *Venus of Willendorf*, ca. 24,000–22,000 BCE, is the first known example of a pregnant figure (new research suggests it may have been made by a woman), it wasn't until the twentieth century that female artists had the platform to tackle in their art what has been historically marginalized, relegated as forbidden, or misidentified as pornographic—as in works by Frida Kahlo (*Henry Ford Hospital*, 1932; fig. 1), Louise Bourgeois (*UNTITLED [WOMAN GIVING BIRTH]*, 1941; fig. 2), Alice Neel (*Pregnant Maria*, 1964), and Senga Nengudi (*R.S.V.P. I*, 1977/2003), and more recently by Clarity Haynes (*Blood Altar*, 2023; fig. 3), Carmen Winant (*My Birth*, 2018), and Luchita Hurtado (*Birthing series*, 2018–20; fig. 4).

Space Between is presented across three galleries. The first room brings together eleven paintings from several series dating from 2016–22, tracking the evolution of Hollowell's techniques and lexicon. Works in this gallery orbit sex, sensualism, and pregnancy in subtle and striking relief. A more intimate gallery spotlights a chronological display of twenty works on paper from 2013–23. Never-before-exhibited, they are all from the artist's archive and in concert demonstrate how Hollowell uses drawing not only to create studies for paintings, but also as a visual diary, memorializing impressions and events on a given day, so that she can move forward while looking back. The third and largest gallery highlights new and recent works, from 2021–23, including the debut of two significant new paintings: one comprises six small works, each incorporating a single cast third-trimester nipple; the other stars an overstated pregnant belly along with five large-scale pastels on paper. This installation reveals time's enactment, its extension and tightening on the prenatal and postpartum body.

The eldest of four siblings, Hollowell was born in 1983 in St. Peter, Minnesota, and raised in Northern California in the agricultural town of Woodland, twenty miles outside Sacramento. The area is known for its fertile soil and its countryside, which Hollowell describes as "laser-leveled flat fields ... [with] huge open skies."[8] Her father, the hyper-figurative painter David Hollowell, taught at UC Davis with artists Wayne Thiebaud, Roy De Forest, and Robert Arneson. Her mother, Terry Hollowell, is a seamstress who studied the graphic arts and worked at one time as a political cartoonist. She also made her children's clothes and now designs black-light reactive clothing for herself and friends for the Burning Man festival in Nevada, which she has long attended.[9] Hollowell attributes the expressive range of her palette not only to the sharp light of Northern California but also to her parents. As she states, "The colors I use in my paintings always fluctuate between the intensely saturated neon hues inspired by my mom and the natural tones my dad prefers."[10] But it was her mother's strong encouragement, when Hollowell was a teenager, to embrace her burgeoning sexuality that gave her the confidence to make it an inflection point in her artistic practice.[11] In high school, Hollowell aspired to be a fashion designer, but she went on to study sculpture in the creative arts department at UC Santa Barbara, where she "made sculptural, performative dresses" that she would wear around campus.[12] After graduating in 2005, she went to New York, was employed as an art handler, and made work out of her small apartment at night. She was accepted to Virginia Commonwealth University's MFA program and while there made "cartoony figurative paintings of people and plants"[13] that were more generally about "the female body and sexuality."[14] In 2012 she received her graduate degree and moved back to New York.

Less than a year later, in 2013, her practice took a prominent swerve after she had an abortion. Two graphite drawings, *Happy Vagina* and

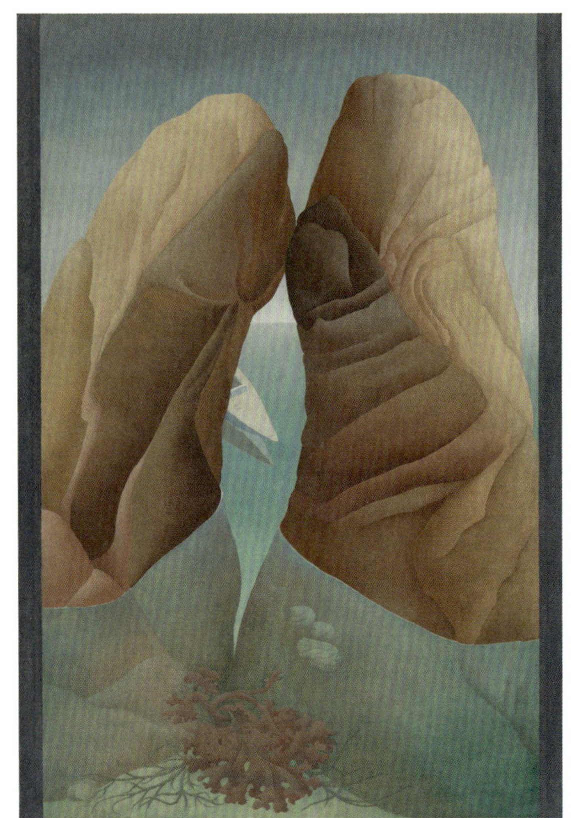
FIG. 5

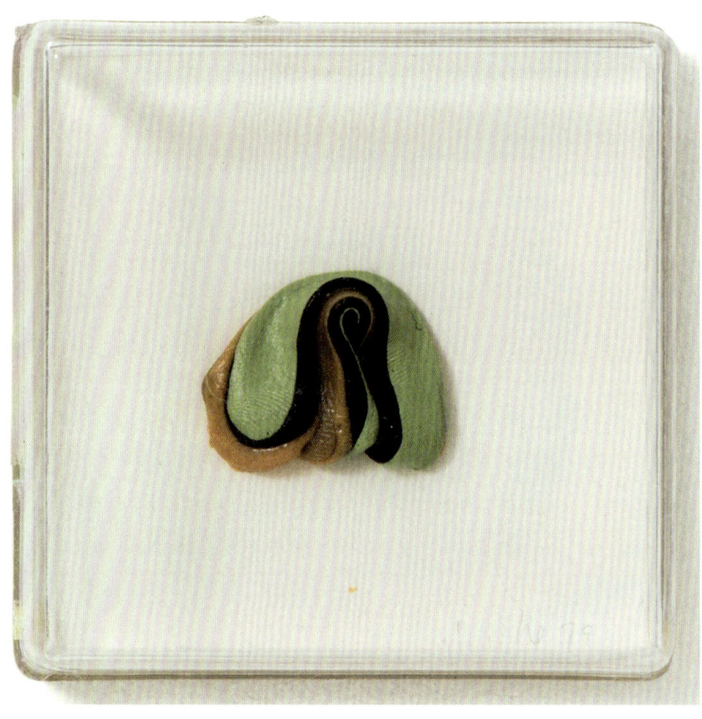
FIG. 7

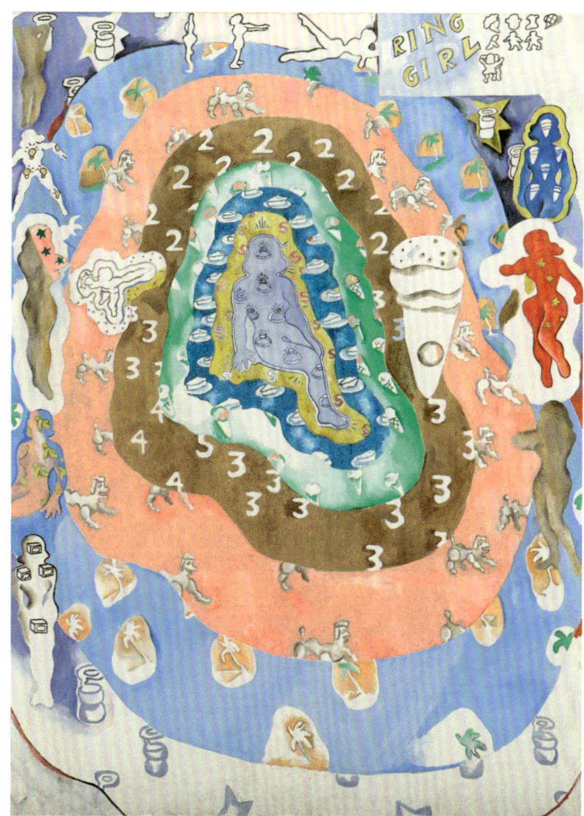

FIG. 6

5. Ithell Colquhoun
Scylla, 1938

6. Suellen Rocca
Ring Girl, c. 1965

7. Hannah Wilke
Untitled, 1979

Emerald Mountain (plates 19, 20), exhibited here for the first time, were created a few months after the procedure.[15] For *Emerald Mountain*, Hollowell transfigured her vagina into a numinous landscape with valleys and mountains that ascend toward an elysian gleam. The double imaging of the female anatomy with the natural world, which is also captured in the later *Yellow Mountains* and *Mountainscape*, both 2016 (plates 11, 28), brings to mind the British surrealist, poet, and author Ithell Colquhoun's preternatural paintings, particularly *Scylla* from 1938 (fig. 5), as well as American modernist Georgia O'Keeffe's "vulvar flowers" and curvaceous hills. The humor evidenced in *Happy Vagina* evokes the graphite and colored-pencil drawings of Chicago imagist Suellen Rocca, whose visualizations were stirred by dreams, Egyptian hieroglyphics, and consumerism with a stress on female anatomy and the hyperfeminine (fig. 6). Hollowell's *Happy Vagina* resembles a pair of clasped hands in prayer, voicing gratitude for her freedom to choose. From then onward, Hollowell decided to center her work on herself, mining the "explosions of pleasure and explosions of pain"[16] in her body and mind through abstraction. Her first mature paintings, from 2014, were all nine by thirteen inches—"the size," she says, "of the area of my vagina and ovaries, my female core area."[17] These works, such as *Circle, Oval, Hairy Mound, Subterranean Eruption,* and *V* (plates 1, 2, and 3), are about orgasm and penetration, menstruation and ovulation—cycles and events specific to female-identifying experiences, with a nod to Judy Chicago's "central core" paintings and Hannah Wilke's gum vaginas, both from the 1970s (fig. 7).

In 2015 Hollowell had her first solo exhibition at the gallery 106 Greene, then located in Brooklyn. She adjusted the scale of her works so they were around the size of her torso. She was abstracting female and male genitalia (hers and her partner's) and replacing it with stylized lingams, ogees, and mandorlas (for example, *Linked Lingams in Green, Purple and Red, Fire Line,* and *Concentric Vibes in Orange and Blue*, all 2015; plates 5, 6, and 7), imagery she discovered in Neo-Tantric and Tantric art as well as early Christian painting and Gothic and Islamic architecture. She was also studying artists associated with the Transcendental Painting Group,[18] and was specifically drawn to Agnes Pelton, Florence Miller Pierce, and Emil Bisttram. Bisttram's painting *The Flaming One*, 1964 (fig. 8), features a mandorla-like shape with fiery tendrils that extend from a beaming core. But the symbolic almond shape also recalls Ana

Mendieta's evocative *Silueta Series* from 1973–80 (fig. 9), in which she merged her body with the land through a series of solitary actions involving burning, impressing, and sculpting. Like Hollowell's images, Mendieta's ephemeral silhouettes couple the earthly with the sacred.

As Hollowell went further inward, directing her attention toward illustrating her and her husband's intercourse, and her own sexual pleasure and fertility, she not only intensified her expanding vocabulary but enhanced her surfaces too, using sawdust and collaging shapes cut from high-density foam to intimate private areas of their bodies, as seen in *Point of Entry (blue green mounds over yellow sky)*, *Point of Entry (lingam between red circles)*, and *The Lands Part (blue, red and purple)*, all 2017 and all forty-eight by thirty-six inches (plates 12, 13, and 14). In *The Lands Part (blue, red and purple)*, Hollowell masqueraded labia as steep and narrow gorges that rise subtly in low relief, while in *Point of Entry (lingam between red circles)*, a bulging shaft transfigures into a beam of shooting light. Her pastel drawings are more explicit, with naughty titles such as *Giving Head*, February 3, 2015, and *Pushed out by dicks*, February 2016 (plates 22, 26), and playful editorializing in the margins. For example, in *Space Between (from one end to the other)*, April 9, 2017 (plate 31), the source for this exhibition's title, Hollowell notes: "Bring out bright pink-yellow flesh color in the Dick—set against the white of the light stream." She is exposing her jumps from frisky figuration to dazzling abstraction.

She also began experimenting with different procedures and applications of paint, exercising a whirling "wrist technique" to picture pubic hair and adding "stippled textures" using the scrubby side of a dish sponge to produce a "thick carpet of paint,"[19] perceptible in the pulpy blood-red discs of *Point of Entry (lingam between red circles)*. She proffers that her "painting surface has a skin to it,"[20] an idea that hints at feminist artists working in the 1960s and 1970s, such as Zilia Sánchez and Harmony Hammond (figs. 10, 11), who used shaped canvases and hand-shaped armatures to produce bumps and curves in a rebuke to painting's patriarchal legacy.

Guided by the Light and Space artists, Hollowell requires her observers to move around her works as they radiate and absorb light. Like Helen Pashgian (fig. 12), who pioneered the use of epoxies and resins

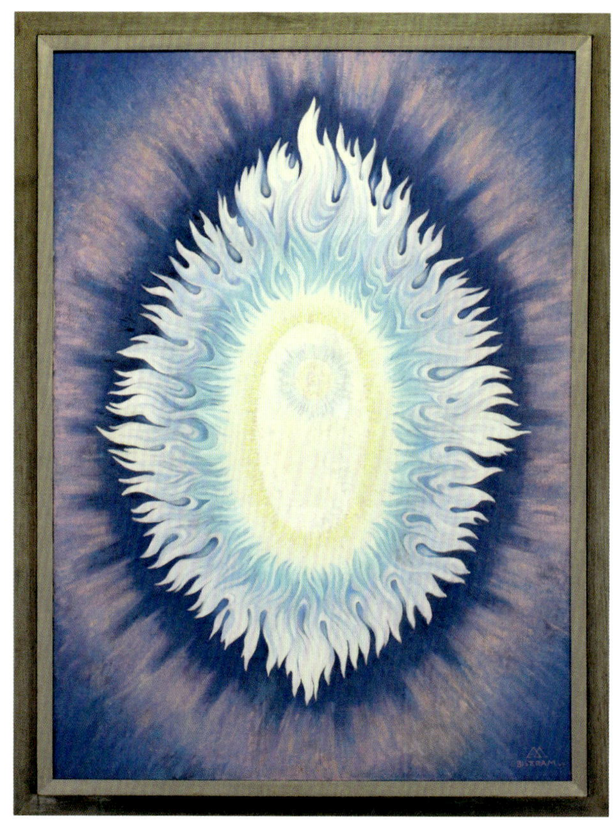

FIG. 8

FIG. 11

8. Emil James Bisttram *The Flaming One*, 1964

9. Ana Mendieta *Untitled: Silueta Series, Iowa*, 1976–78

10. Zilia Sánchez *Las Amazonas* [The Amazons], 1968

11. Harmony Hammond *Green*, 1976

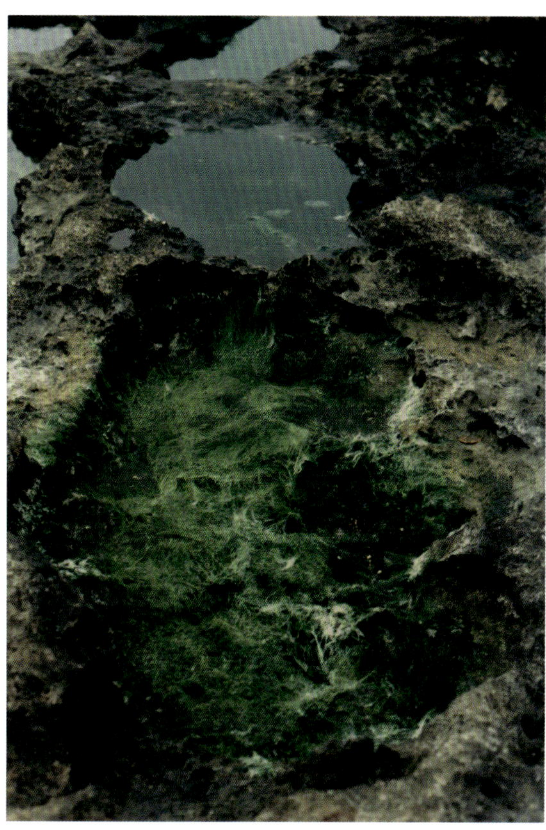

FIG. 9

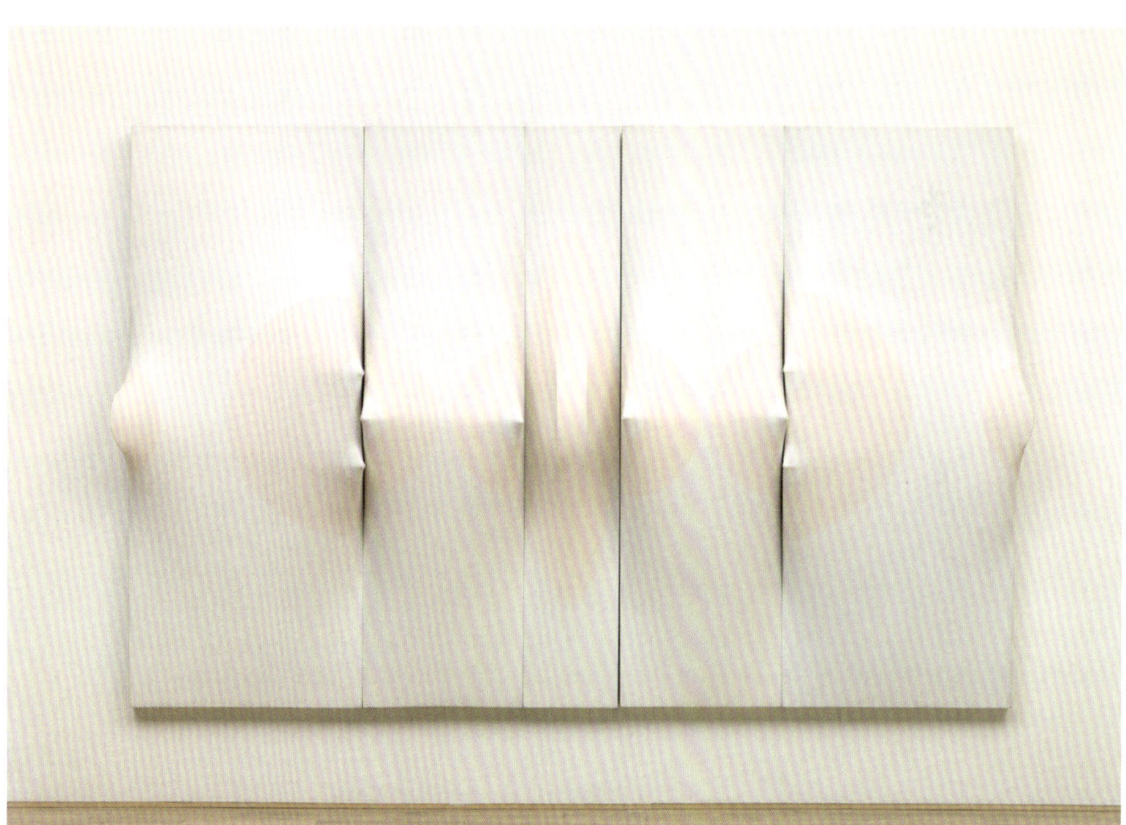

FIG. 10

to produce polished orbs and discs in translucent colors, Hollowell's paintings are optical and performative too, doing what Pashgian has articulated as the "perception and the phenomenon of really having an experience, not just an observation."[21] Hollowell's works surprise viewers with their demanding physicality, variable dimensionality, and ocular impact; they expect to be seen and sensed.

With time Hollowell advanced the scale of her paintings, but always in relation to her own body. The works in the *Plumb Line* series from 2019 measure six by four and a half feet, with sections that float about two inches off the panels. Their size, Hollowell concedes, approximates her upright frame with arms extended. There are three works from the series in the exhibition: *Prenatal Plumb Line, Red Hole,* and *Standing in yellow, pink and blue* (plates 15, 16, and 17). She acknowledges that these paintings are about pregnancy and postpartum, representing the body's alterations for a growing fetus and realignments after the baby is born, reducing the artist to a sequence of "stacked parts"[22] that she then reconfigured over many iterations. Hollowell first experimented with this idea three years earlier, before having children, in *Full Frontal* (*in Green*), 2016 (plate 8), which measures four by three feet. In *Prenatal Plumb Line*, Hollowell's figure doubles as a metronome. The artist says that she concentrates on three basic forms: an oval for her head; semicircles for breasts, pregnant belly, and buttock; and the mandorla for her vulva. Each shape is CNC (computer numerical control) milled from high-density foam and fastened to the linen-wrapped panels. The paintings' emphatic color schemes, stringent frontality, and two-to-three-dimensionality reference salon cubism but more insistently relate to the paintings of G. R. Santosh (fig. 13), who has said: "I divide the canvas down the central axis and start. Since I try to create colour as light, the painting is built slowly, gradually."[23] Likewise, Hollowell applies a rigid vertical or horizontal setup. She crafts a "stream of light"[24] that slices down the middle of the body and bisects it to signify the vertebral column or chi, the life dynamism that flows from each of us. Her colors rage and flush, characterizing her moods at different times, the memories of which she has recorded in pastel studies that guide her choices.

Hollowell also mines the impact of pure abstraction, as seen explicitly in several works in the exhibition: the painting *Split Orbs in teal and mauve*, 2021; the painting *Scarlet Brain*, 2022; and the pastel-on-paper *Overview Effect*, February 14, 2023 (plates 18, 42, and 46). The *Split Orb* series, 2021–present, flanks the deliveries of her two children. Hollowell distills the explosive agony of childbirth, what she portrays as the "sensation of my brain and my belly splitting open,"[25] into cleaving orbs that feel out of this world. Vivid perceptions of distress and reverence, her imaginings also insinuate a cellular division, or more spectacularly a planetary split. Hollowell's heavenly color haze, exemplified in *Split Orbs in teal and mauve,* rushes from center to margins, a palpable embodiment that suggests a cosmic happening.

"Overview effect" is a term used to define the awestruck impression an astronaut has while viewing Earth from space. In Hollowell's *Overview Effect*, two flaming lenses transect. Beaming at their crossing is a golden mandorla encircled by a palpitating, prismatic halo. Her composition summons to mind the exalted simplicity of Agnes Pelton's *Departure*, 1952, which pictures two light-filled rings converging at sunset, perhaps a redolent convening of the living and the heavenly. Hollowell discloses that her pair epitomize "life pre- and post-motherhood, with the ovals symbolizing the time before and time after becoming a parent."[26] Her *Brain* series from 2022 was made in response to an acute head injury her father suffered after a fall, resulting in his inability to speak or write. *Scarlet Brain* (plate 42) echoes the earlier *Red Hole*, as a portrait of a flaming red ovoid here fills almost the entire composition. If it could enounce a sound, it would be a resonant "om." A horizontal bar hems the bottom edge, referencing a scroll and a horizon line for the brain to rest on.[27] Hollowell's creation is reminiscent of the visual devices used by Tantric practitioners to meditate and calm the psyche (fig. 14).

While the artist was pregnant with her second child, her husband, sculptor Brian Caverly, made a body cast of her pregnant torso as a memento, she says.[28] She had no intention at the time to introduce it into her work. But it soon became a new tool, which broadened into making molds of friends' pregnant bellies and lactating breasts, establishing a tight network of new and expecting mothers. Casting from the molds with Aqua-Resin, Hollowell's studio sands, epoxies, and screws the sculpted body parts to her panels and then covers them with layers of gesso and acrylic medium so they appear embedded or

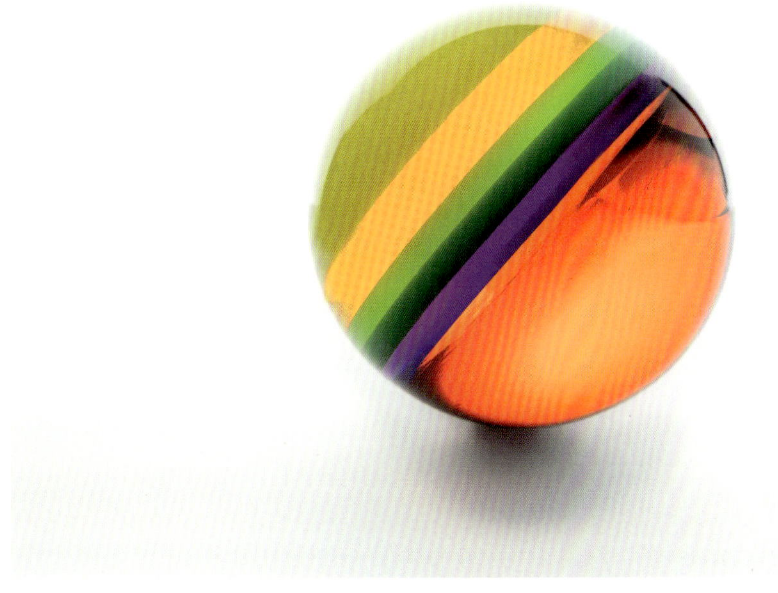

FIG. 12

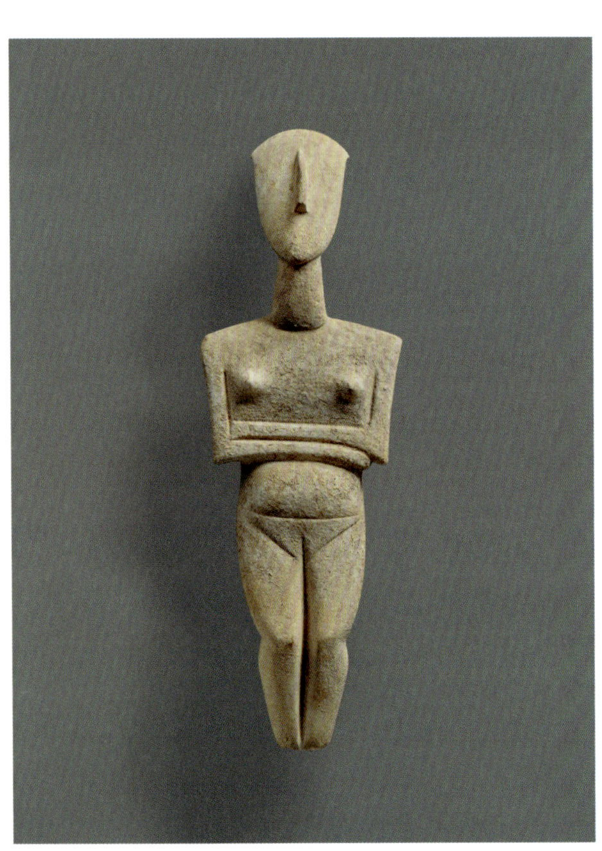

FIG. 15

12. Helen Pashgian
    Untitled, 2020

13. G.R. Santosh
    Shakti vichor, 1982

14. Anonymous
    Untitled, 2000,
    Sanganer & Delhi

15. Attributed to the
    Schuster Master
    (Cycladic, active
    about 2400 B.C.)
    Female Figure of the
    Late Spedos Type,
    about 2400 B.C.

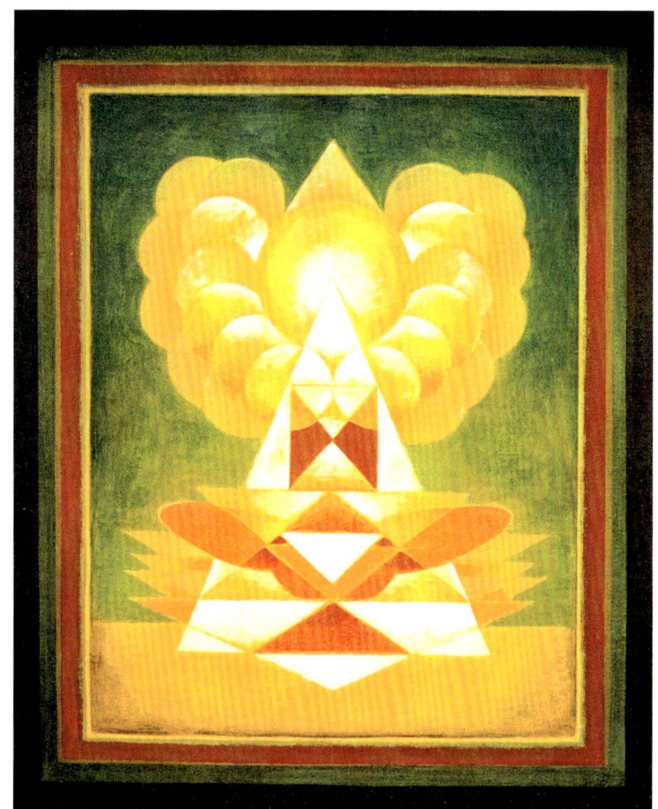
FIG. 13

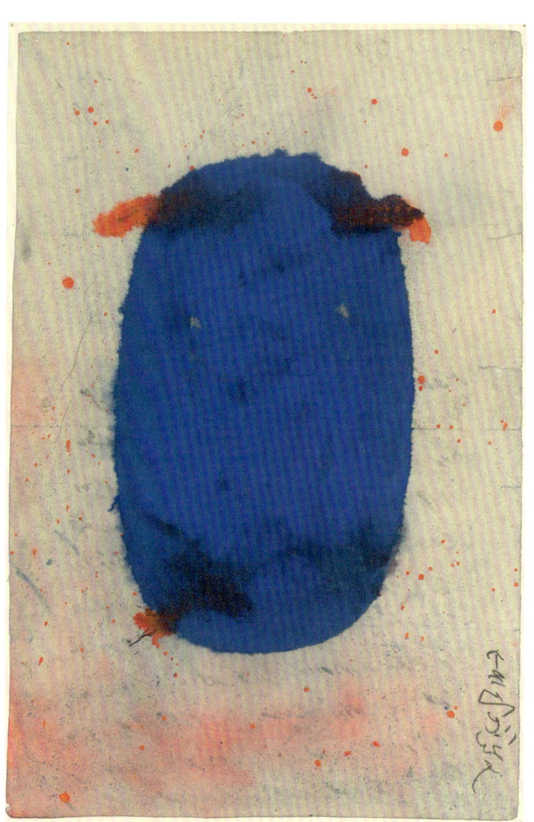
FIG. 14

entombed. Hollowell paints over the surfaces with oil paint. At first, she kept the breasts and bellies within the tonalities of skin, staging them within arrangements that were more subdued than the primary and resplendent hues of past series. One of the initial works encompassing these new methods is the considerable painting *Empty Belly*, 2021 (plate 43). Compressing time, Hollowell condenses pregnancy and maternity into one frame. It features a third-trimester belly perched above a much bigger, flat, black void, a depiction of an empty womb. A newborn's small hands reach out toward an arc of engorged breasts.

Breastfeeding first made an appearance in Hollowell's work in 2016 with the pastel-on-paper *Boob Wheel* (plate 29). Since becoming a mother, Hollowell has made the lactating breast a central character, addressing a subject that is sorely lacking in our visual culture. For instance, the small painting *Tick-Tock Belly Clock*, 2021 (plate 38), is a mossy green-gray-yellow, a color associated with the natural world as seen in the 2013 painting *Emerald Mountain* (plate 4). Connecting earth's fertility to a mother's milk, Hollowell endowed her configuration with two pairs of swollen breasts that seem flipped, making them familiar and strange. Small light-filled orbs and running lines that evoke squirting milk form pendulums that swing between the perky pair, a nod to nursing's duration and labor. Hollowell monumentalizes and honors a mothers' life-sustaining superpower, while also acknowledging the exhaustion and discomfort it brings.

Now a few years removed from the births of her two children, Hollowell is considering those events from a distance. Her newest experimentations merge the animated color patterns seen in her prior bodies of work with the more visceral realism of her breast and belly casts. *11pm, 1am, 3am, 5am, 7am, 9am*, 2023 (plate 48), is a series of six small paintings that from afar read like apertures of fugitive color: their seriality alludes to minimalism, particularly the spectrum paintings of Ellsworth Kelly, but with a feminist twist. The canvases, which simulate the scale of a windowpane, swing from nighttime blues to sunrise mauves and early morning yellows. But up close, a single nipple inhumed under layers of oil paint surges to the surface. Divorced from its pair, it conjures a lunarscape, miniaturized volcano, or tiny island. Installed nearby is Hollowell's largest pastel on paper, *10pm Feeding - Around the Clock*, December 5, 2022 (plate 41), the inspiration for the tonal scales captured in *11pm, 1am, 3am, 5am, 7am, 9am*. An immense sundial, it is based on the memory of a sizable wall clock that hung in Hollowell's childhood kitchen. Double life-size breasts, occupied with milk, are stand-ins for each hour, dappled to correspond with a specific time of day.

For her newest body of work, called *In Transition,* from 2023, Hollowell assures that she is "impregnating her paintings!"[29] Part of a larger series of ten paintings that depict the effacement and dilation of the cervix from zero to ten centimeters during labor (unveiled in *Eight Centimeters Dilated in purple, blue, red and yellow*, 2023, plate 47), these works were spurred by her second child's home birth in a bathtub.[30] Hollowell has imparted each painting with a larger-than-life-size nine-month belly. Like a giant balloon, it looks fleshy and smooth, popping off at a depth of more than seven inches. These works, Hollowell explains, are informed by that uncanny feeling "of being both outside the body and then instantly sucked back into yourself"[31] during childbirth. Or what Mina Loy enounces in her 1914 poem *Parturition*: "I am the centre / Of a circle of pain / Exceeding its boundaries in every direction."[32] Each belly is rendered in a brilliant shade, from unclouded yellows to hot-blooded reds, from voltaic magentas to stormy purples and majestic blues. The bellies elicit moons and suns and are encircled by "radiating energy lines"[33] that visualize the rippling spectacle of labor's intensity and escalating pain. Below each belly, Hollowell has rendered fleshy red and pink circles, personifying the exact size of the cervix as it opens.[34] Like twenty-first-century updates on the marble Cycladic figurines of pregnant women from the Bronze Era (fig. 15), these works venerate the trauma and wonder of labor, styling the artist's own mother goddesses.

With the fall of *Roe v. Wade* and the persistent attack on female-identifying bodily autonomy, Hollowell's work is all the more necessary and urgent *because* it is so personal and generous, bringing communities of women together to commemorate their agency and strength. Hollowell declares, "Motherhood never leaves you. … I'll forever be processing it."[35] But we can hope that as she enters her next life stage, her energy and ingenuity will turn toward another topic glaringly absent in contemporary art—the maturing body—because facing harrowing change is the highest marker of our power.

1. Excerpted from Loy's poem "Parturition" (1914), in *The Lost Lunar Baedeker: Poems of Mina Loy*, ed. Roger L. Conover (New York: Farrar, Straus and Giroux, 1996), 7.
2. Bourgeois quoted in Jennifer Peltz, "Sculptor Louise Bourgeois Plumbed Depths of Female Psyche, Made Giant Freaky Spiders," *Christian Science Monitor*, June 1, 2010, https://www.csmonitor.com/From-the-news-wires/2010/0601/Sculptor-Louise-Bourgeois-plumbed-depths-of-female-psyche-made-giant-freaky-spiders.
3. An ogee arch has two S-shaped curves that meet at a point.
4. A mandorla is an almond-shaped aureole that surrounds holy figures such as Jesus and the Virgin Mary in early Christian art.
5. A lingam is a symbol for the Hindu god Shiva.
6. Hollowell to the author, email, December 6, 2023.
7. Neo-Tantric art was a painting style in India in the 1960s and 1970s that incorporated visual signs and symbols of Buddhist and Hindu Tantrism. Tantra is a yogic tradition developed in India that employs mantras or chants and visual devices called yantras. Tantra devotees believe in the unity of the masculine (the Hindu god Shiva) and the feminine (the Hindu goddess Shakti).
8. Hollowell quoted in Casey Lesser, "Loie Hollowell on Abstraction, Making the Grotesque Beautiful, and Her Latest Work," Artsy, March 14, 2023, https://www.artsy.net/article/artsy-editorial-loie-hollowell-abstraction-making-grotesque-beautiful-latest-work.
9. Hollowell to the author, email, February 14, 2024.
10. Hollowell quoted in Osman Can Yerebakan, "Loie Hollowell on Painting, Pain, and Her Second Birth," *Artforum*, May 26, 2021, https://www.artforum.com/columns/loie-hollowell-on-painting-pain-and-her-second-birth-250015/.
11. Hollowell in Sarah Thornton, "Loie Hollowell on Frottage, Fantasy and Feminist Erotica," *Interview Magazine*, January 23, 2024, https://www.interviewmagazine.com/author/sarah-thornton.
12. Hollowell quoted in Marley Marius, "You'll Want to Pay Close Attention at Loie Hollowell's New Show," *Vogue*, September 13, 2019, https://www.vogue.com/article/loie-hollowell-plumb-line-pace-gallery.
13. Hollowell in an audio clip made for *Loie Hollowell: Space Between, A Survey of Ten Years*, edited by Gloria Perez; https://thealdrich.org/exhibitions/loie-hollowell-a-survey#audio-3.
14. Hollowell quoted in "VCUarts Alum Loie Hollowell Makes a Triumphant Return to Campus," *VCU News*, August 8, 2023, https://news.vcu.edu/article/2023/08/vcuarts-alum-loie-hollowell-makes-a-triumphant-return-to-campus.
15. Hollowell to the author, email, December 18, 2023.
16. Hollowell quoted in Haley Mellin, "Is Loie Hollowell a Georgia O'Keeffe for the Instagram Age?," *GARAGE Magazine*, no. 12 (Spring/Summer 2017), posted January 19, 2020, https://www.vice.com/en/article/j5eyp8/is-loie-hollowell-a-georgia-okeefe-for-the-instagram-age.
17. Hollowell quoted in Mellin, "Is Loie Hollowell a Georgia O'Keeffe for the Instagram Age?"
18. The Transcendental Painting Group was created in 1938 in New Mexico and included artists Emil Bisttram, Ed Garman, Robert Gribbroek, Lawren Harris, Raymond Jonson, William Lumpkins, Florence Miller Pierce, Agnes Pelton, Horace Towner Pierce, and Stuart Walker. According to the group's statement of purpose, "The word 'Transcendental' has been chosen as a name for the group because it best expresses the aims, which are to carry painting beyond the world through new concepts of space, light and design, upon planes that are termed idealistic and spiritual." See Transcendental Painting Group (N.M.), Transcendental Painting Group statement of purpose, 1938?, Agnes Pelton papers, 1885–1989, Archives of American Art, Smithsonian Institution. See also Michael Duncan, ed., *Another World: The Transcendental Painting Group* (Sacramento: Crocker Art Museum; New York: DelMonico Books/D.A.P., 2021).

19. Hollowell quoted in "Form Is Personal: Elissa Auther in Conversation with Loie Hollowell," in *Loie Hollowell: Plumbline* (New York: Pace Gallery, 2019), 98.
20. Hollowell quoted in "Loie Hollowell," *The Great Women Artists Podcast with Katy Hessel*, August 4, 2020, episode 36, https://podcasts.apple.com/gb/podcast/loie-hollowell/id1480259187?i=1000487128022.
21. Helen Pashgian quoted in Canada Choate, "Helen Pashgian on Her Visionary Life in Color," *Artforum*, November 15, 2021, https://www.artforum.com/columns/helen-pashgian-on-her-visionary-life-in-color-250970/.
22. Hollowell quoted in a virtual conversation with Betsy Johnson, "Artist Loie Hollowell on Art and the Female Body," Hirshhorn Museum, March 8, 2023, https://hirshhorn.si.edu/event/artist-loie-hollowell-on-art-and-the-female-body/.
23. G. R. Santosh quoted in Shantiveer Kaul, *The Art of G. R. Santosh* (New Delhi: Roli, 2000), 16.
24. Hollowell quoted in "Form Is Personal," 93.
25. Hollowell quoted in Kristen Knupp, "Loie Hollowell: The Third Stage," *Art Vista*, September 4, 2023, https://art-vista.com/loie-hollowell-the-third-stage/.
26. See note 13.
27. Hollowell in conversation with the author, February 13, 2024.
28. Hollowell in conversation with the author, October 19, 2023.
29. Artist's talk with museum staff during a walk-through of *Loie Hollowell: Space Between, A Survey of Ten Years*, January 18, 2024.
30. Hollowell in conversation with the author, January 18, 2024.
31. Hollowell quoted in Thornton, "Loie Hollowell on Frottage, Fantasy and Feminist Erotica."
32. Loy, "Parturition," 4.
33. Hollowell quoted in Knupp, "Loie Hollowell: The Third Stage."
34. Hollowell to the author, email, February 14, 2024.
35. Hollowell quoted in Kabir Jhala, "Painter Loie Hollowell, Who Is Launching an NFT Series to Support Abortion Funds, Discusses Politics, Motherhood and Her Market," *Art Newspaper*, October 28, 2022, https://www.theartnewspaper.com/2022/10/28/nft-support-us-abortion-funds-loie-hollowell-pace-verso.

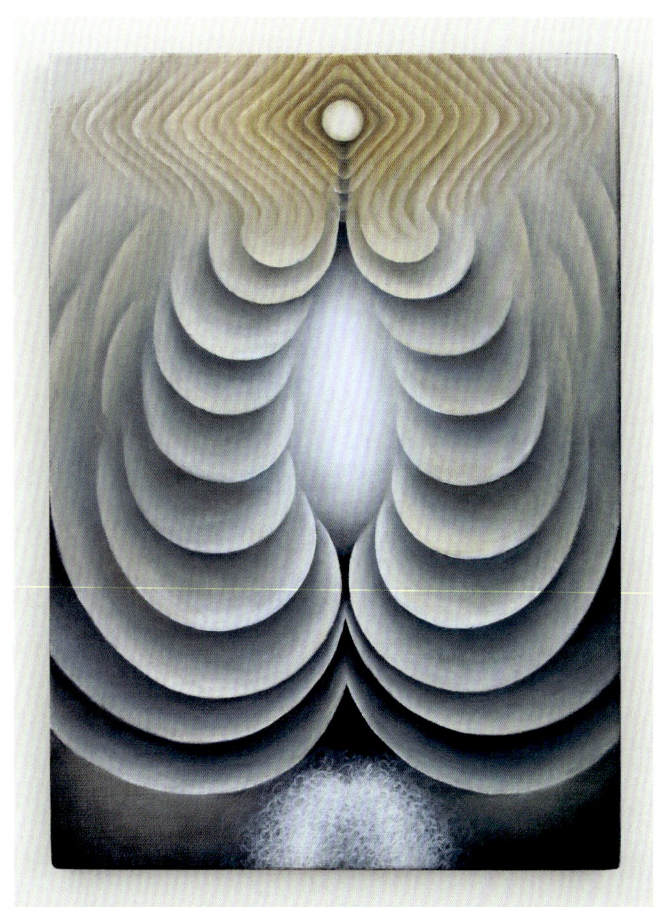

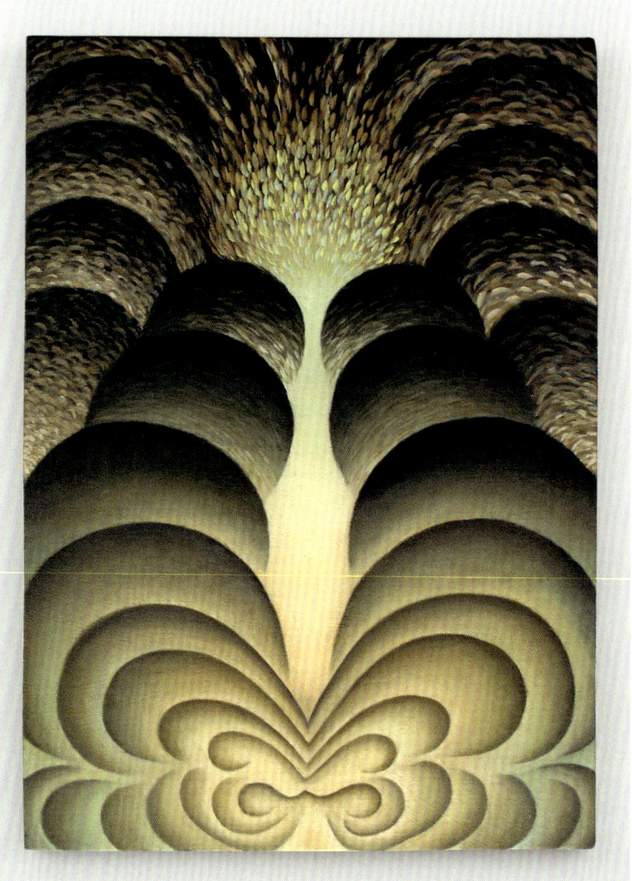

1.
Circle, Oval, Hairy Mound, 2014

2.
Subterranean Eruption, 2014

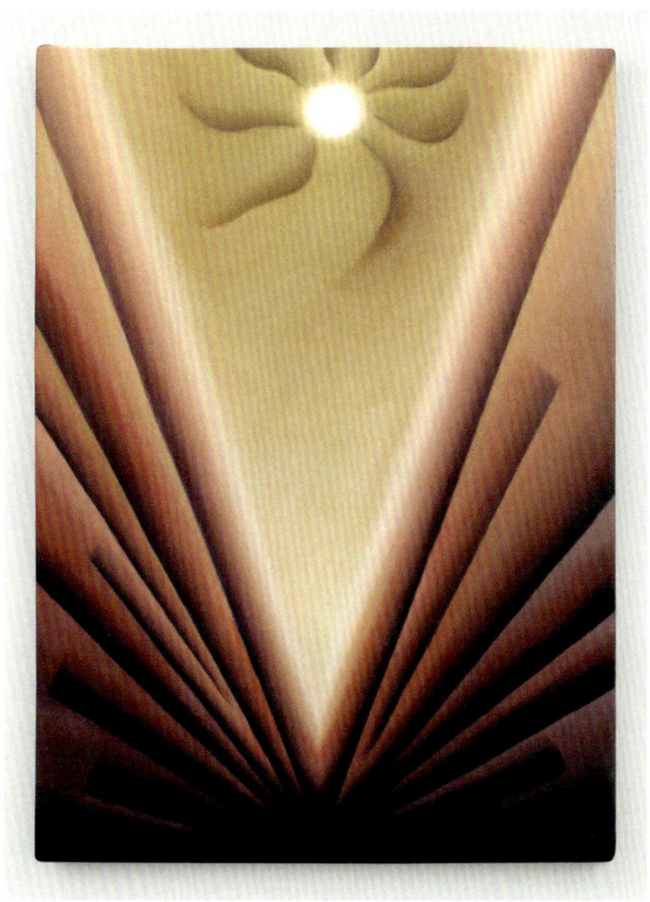

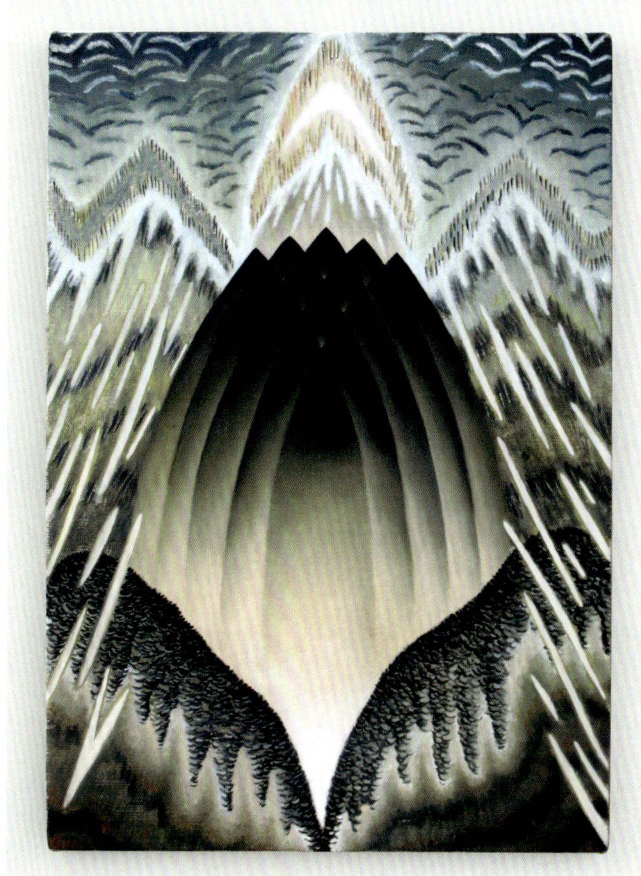

3.
V, 2014

4.
Emerald Mountain, 2014

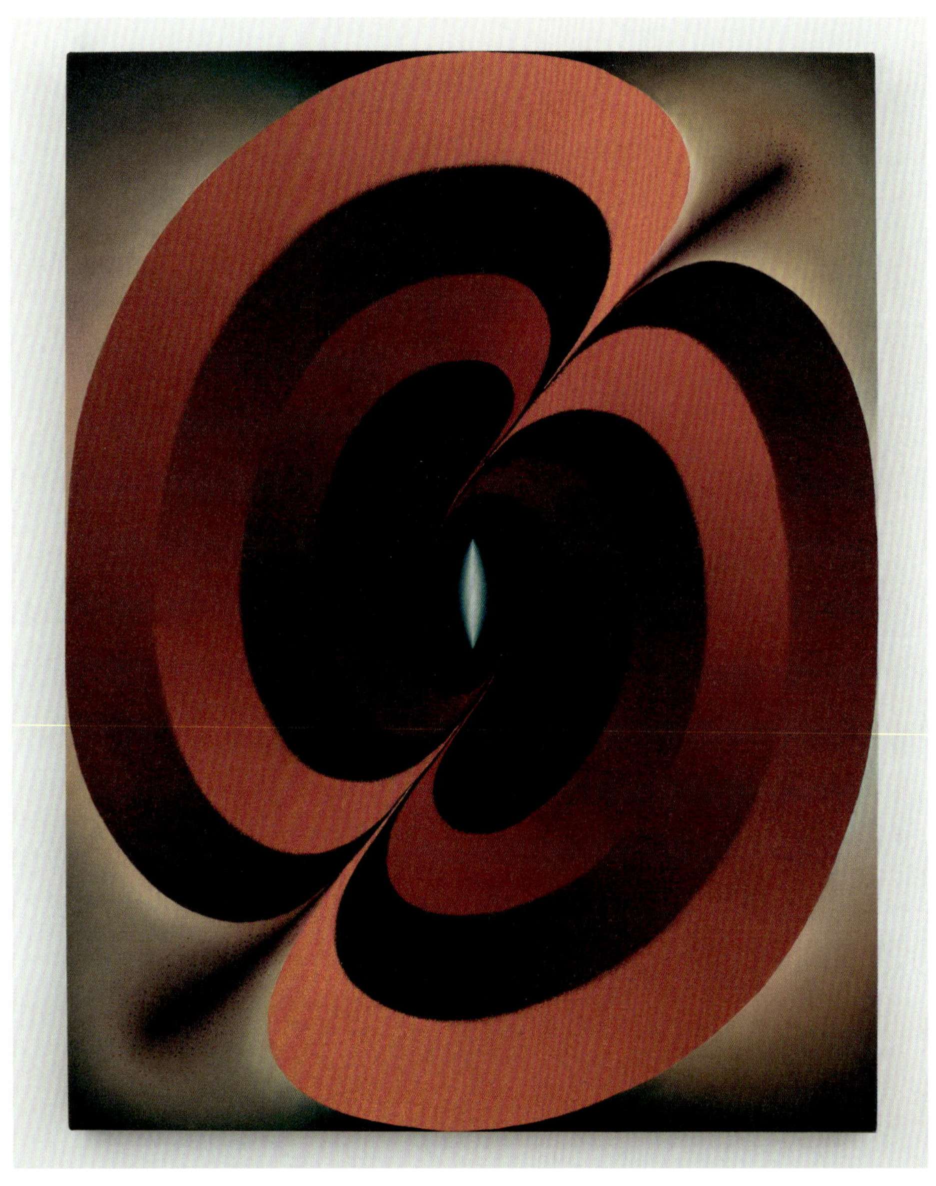

5.
Linked Lingams in Green, Purple and Red, 2015

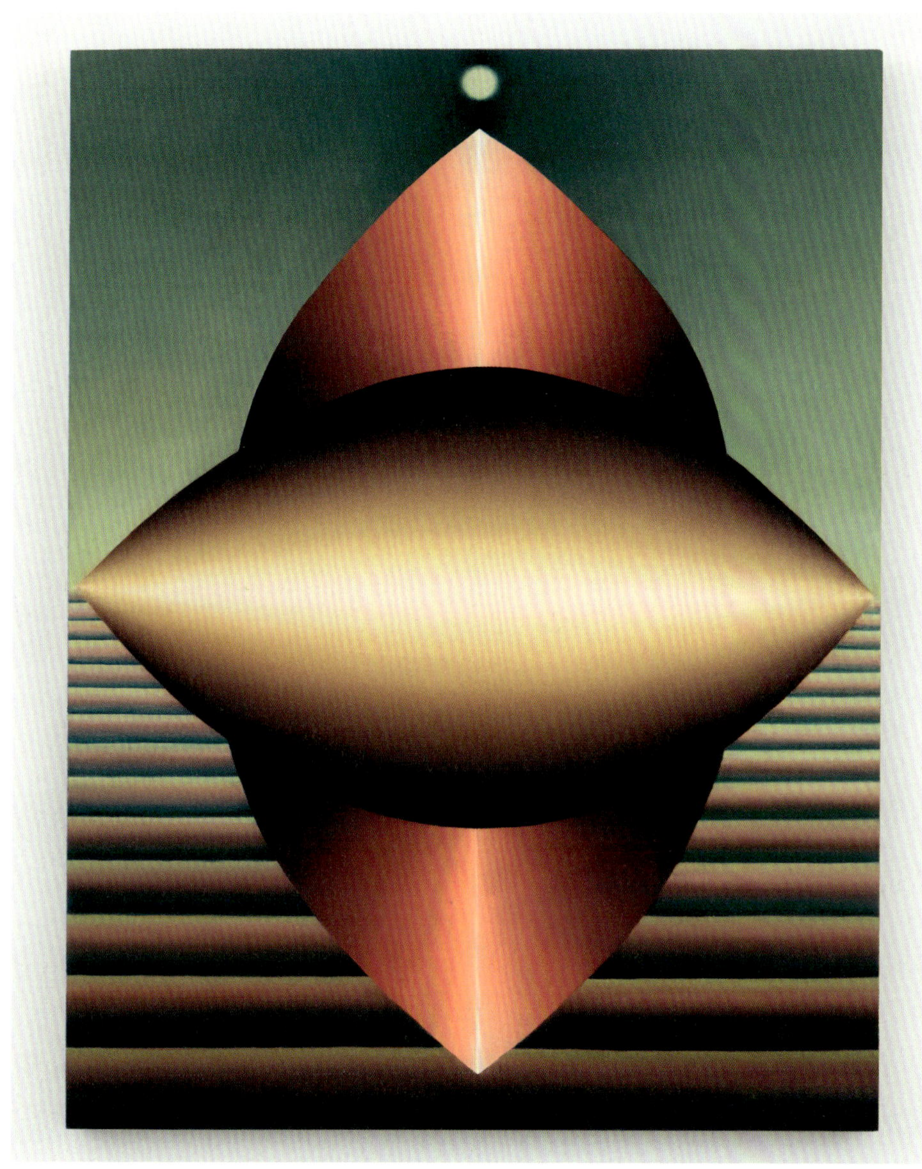

6.
Fire Line, 2015

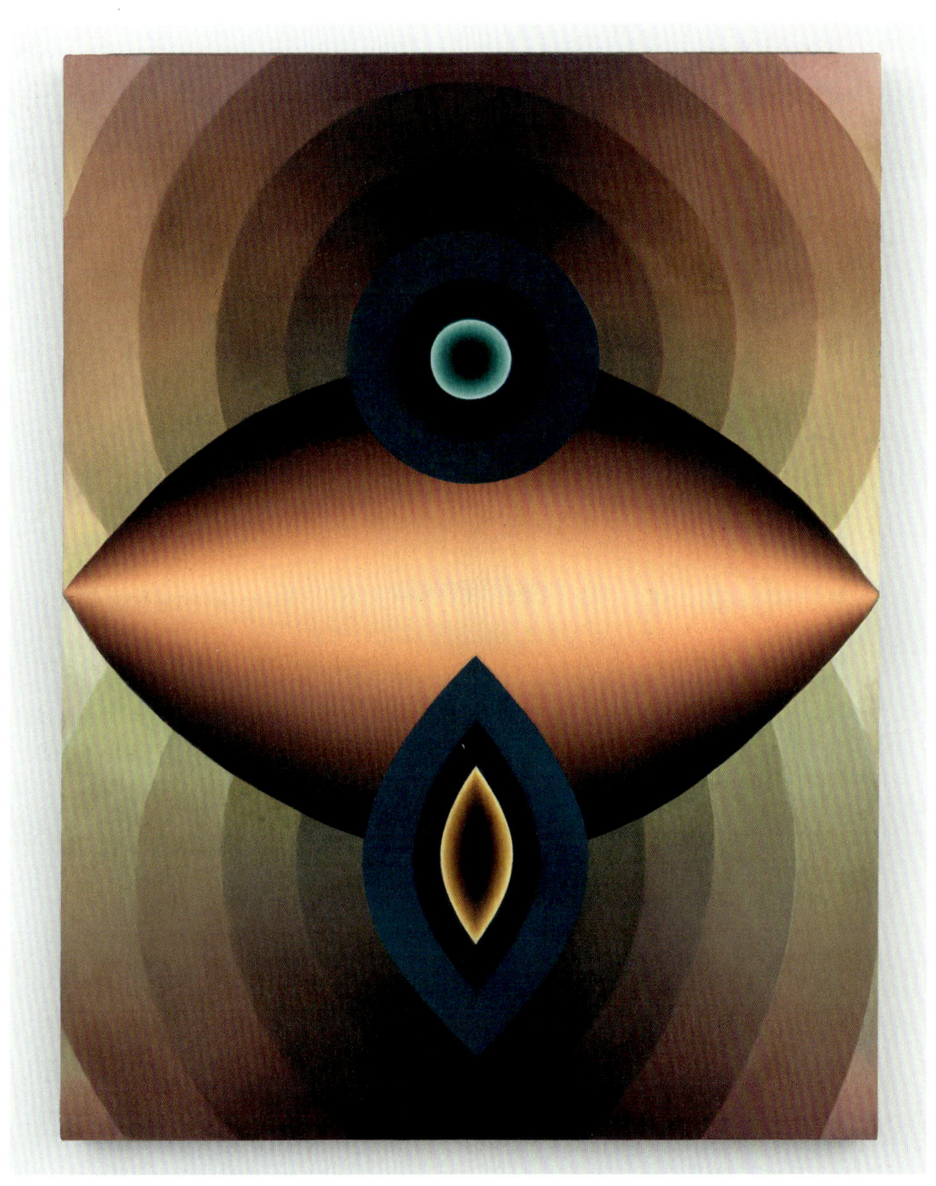

7.
Concentric Vibes in Orange and Blue, 2015

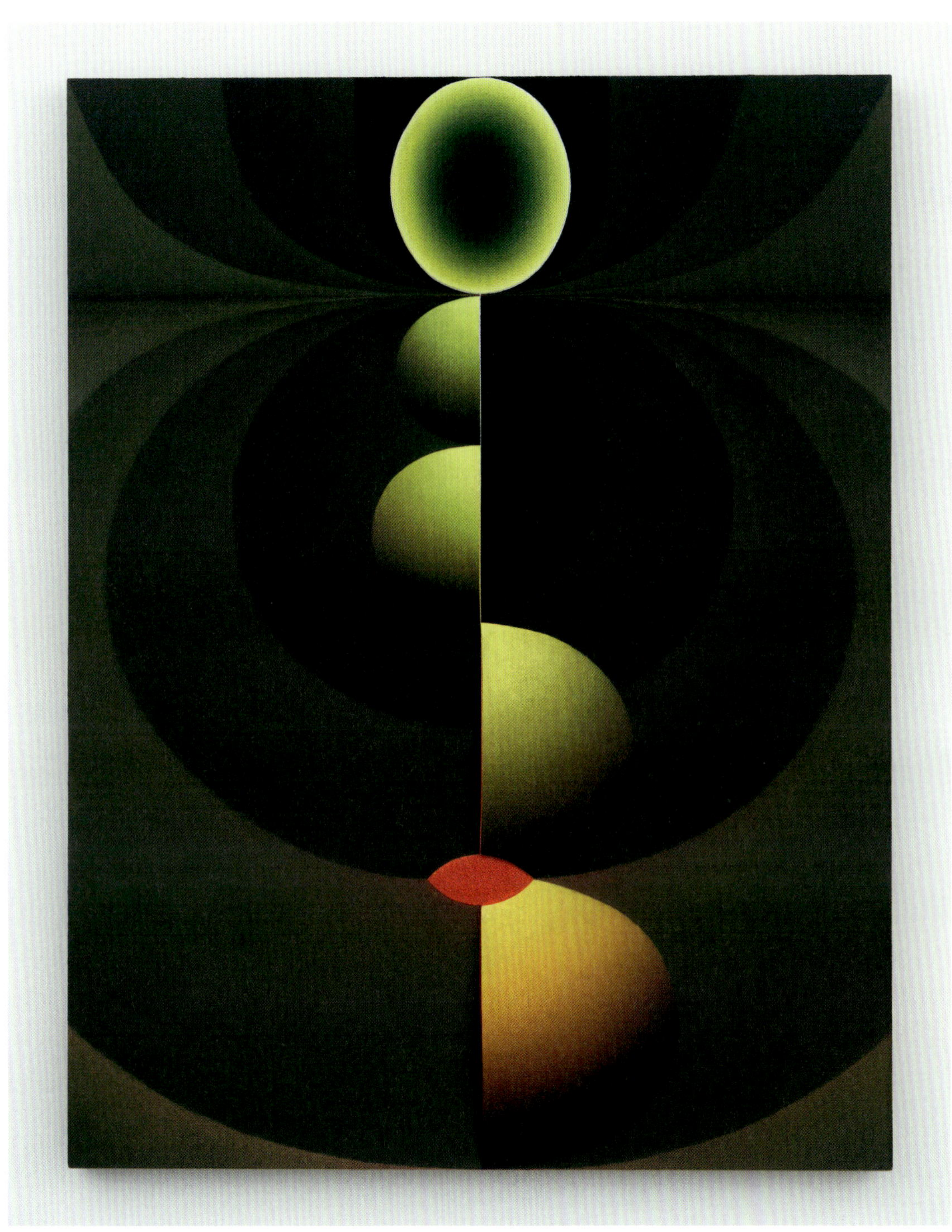

8.
Full Frontal (in Green), 2016

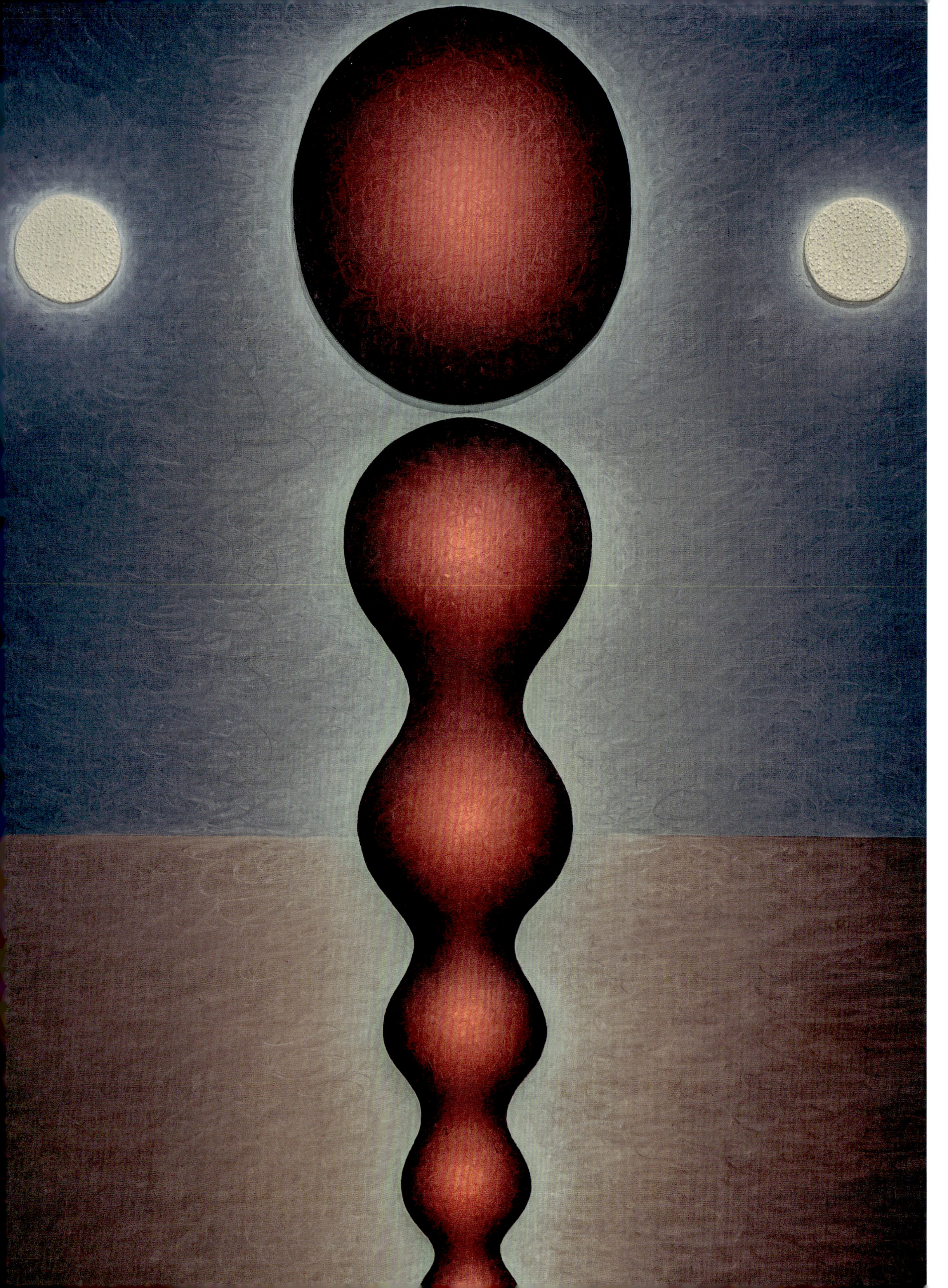

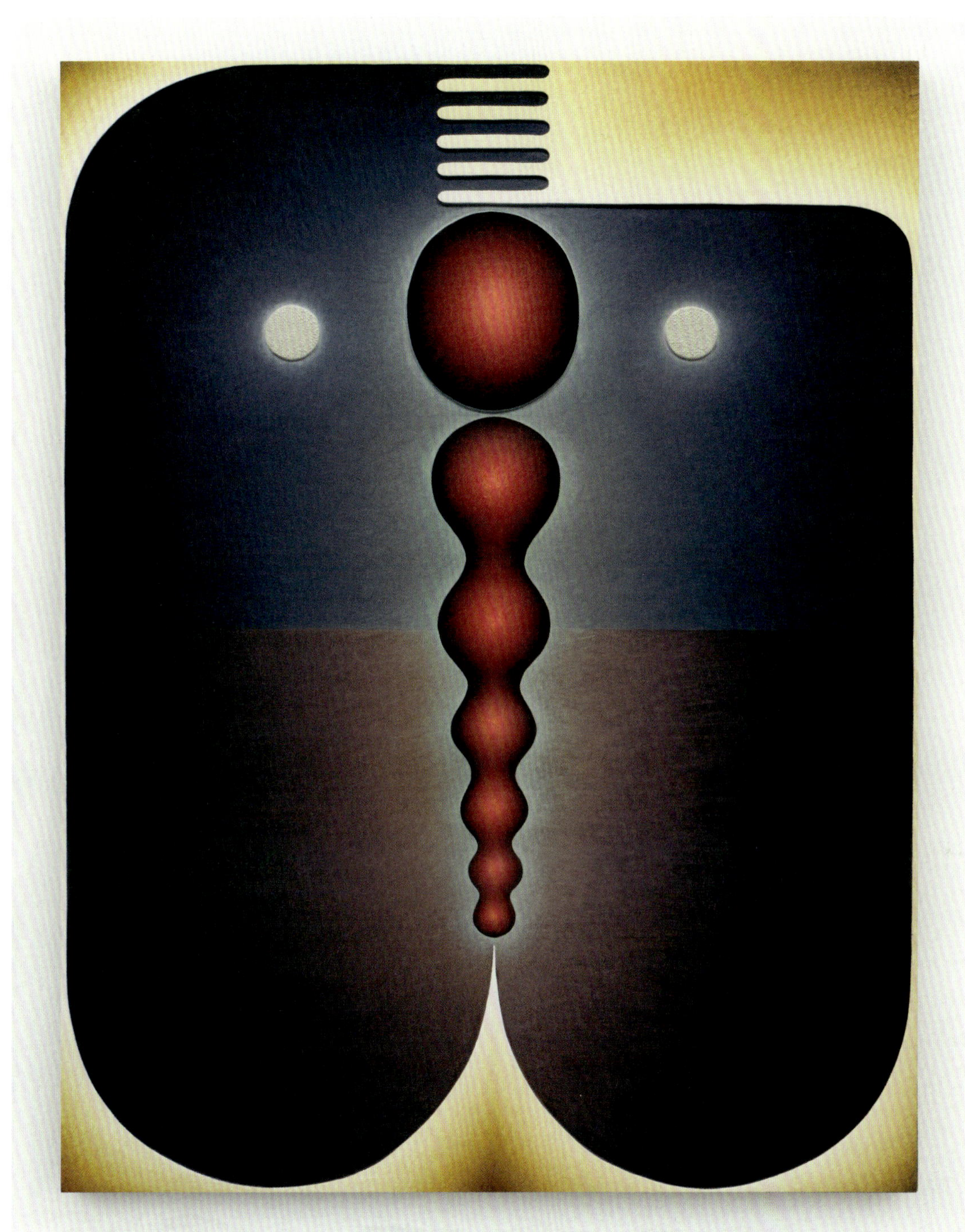

9.
Body of Water (in Yellow), 2016

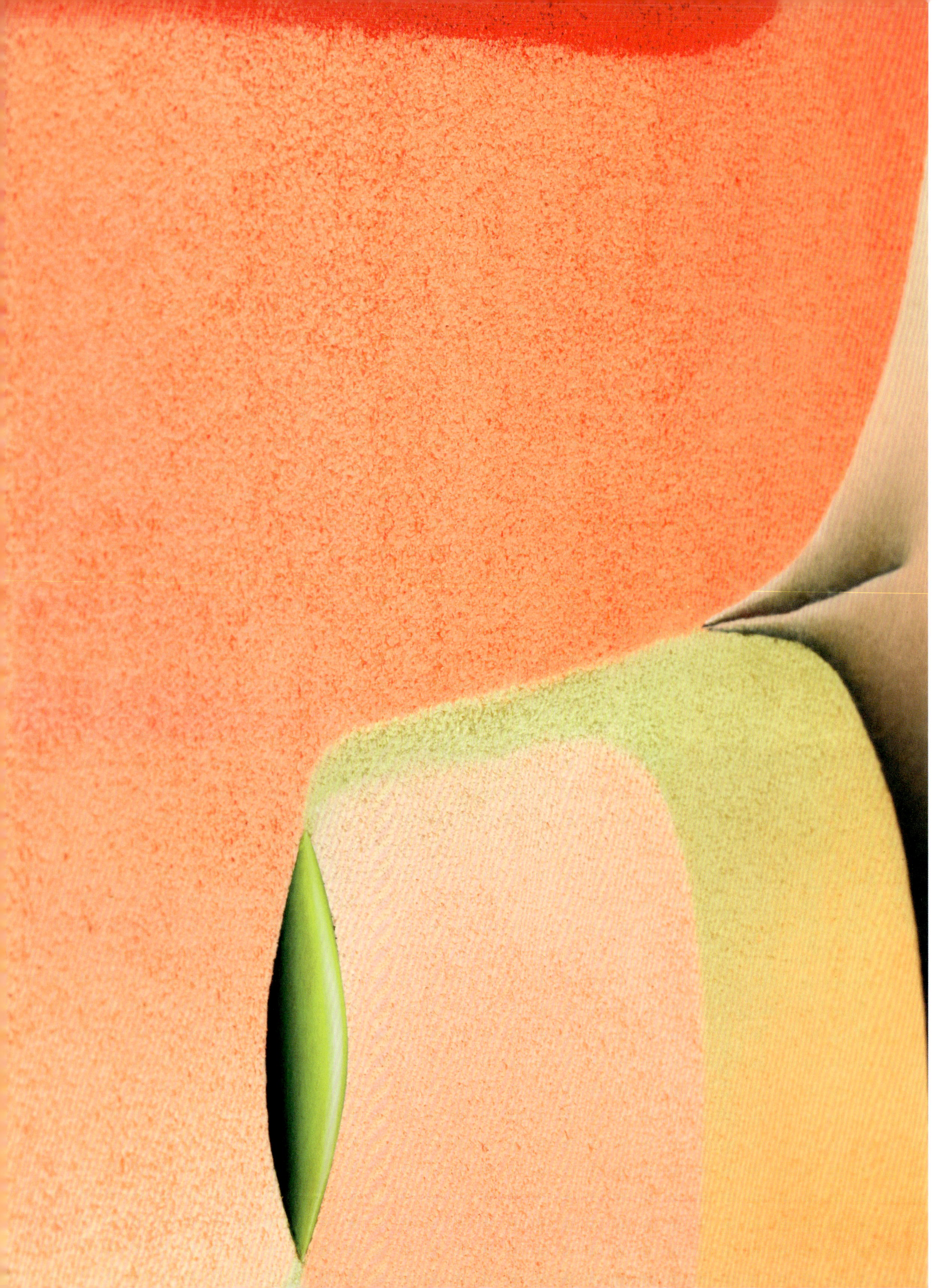

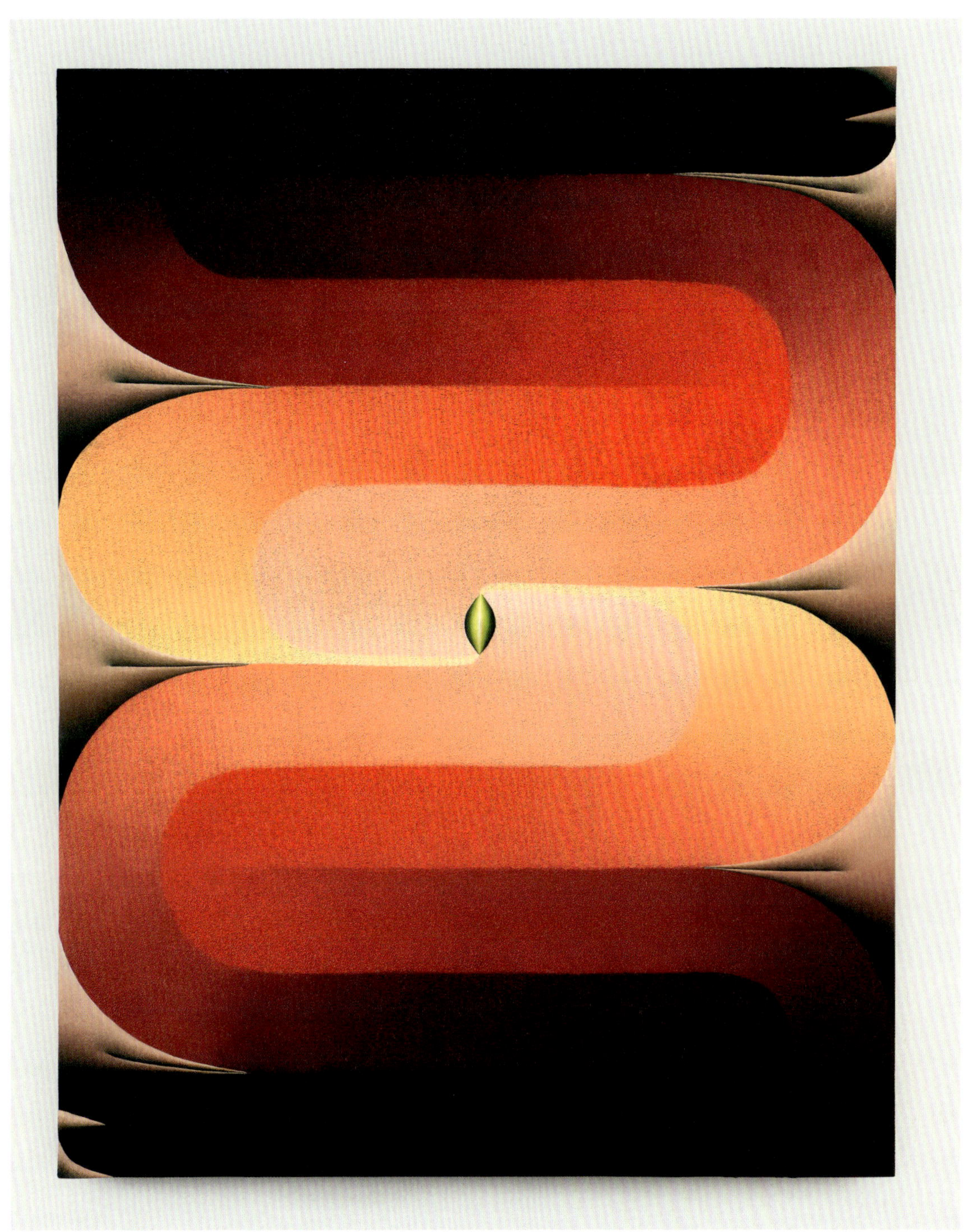

10.
Stacked Lingam in red, yellow, purple and green, 2016

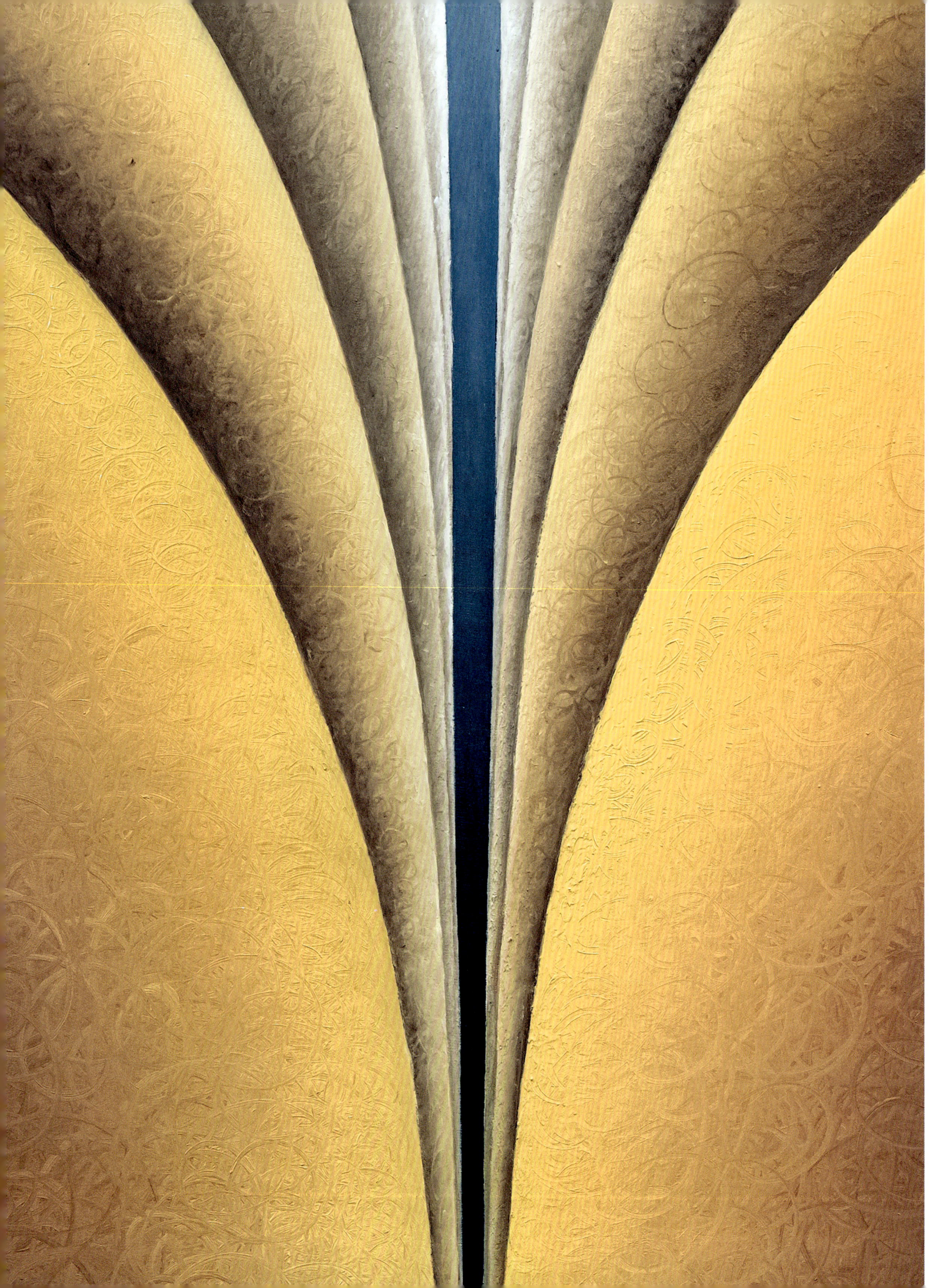

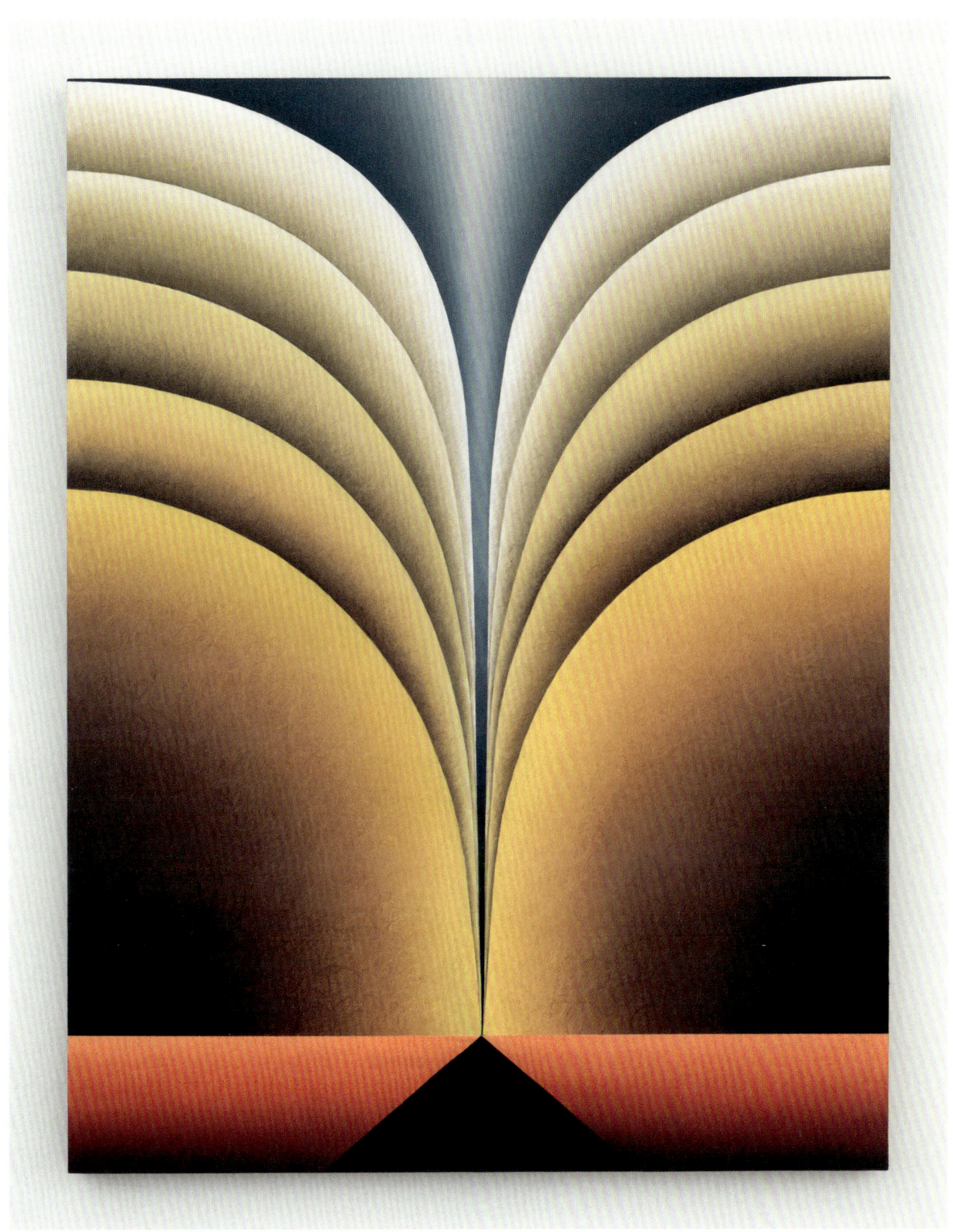

11.
Yellow Mountains, 2016

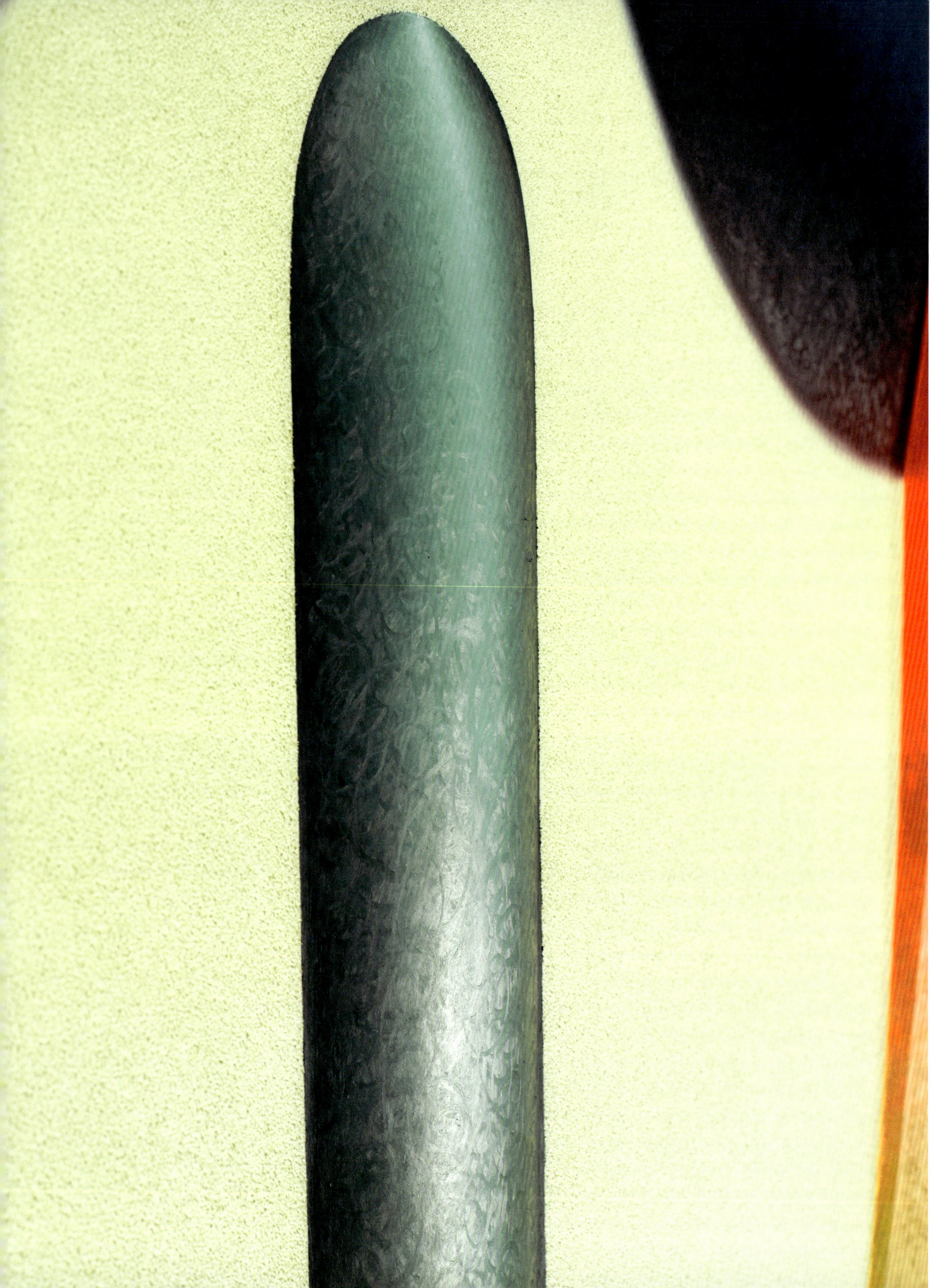

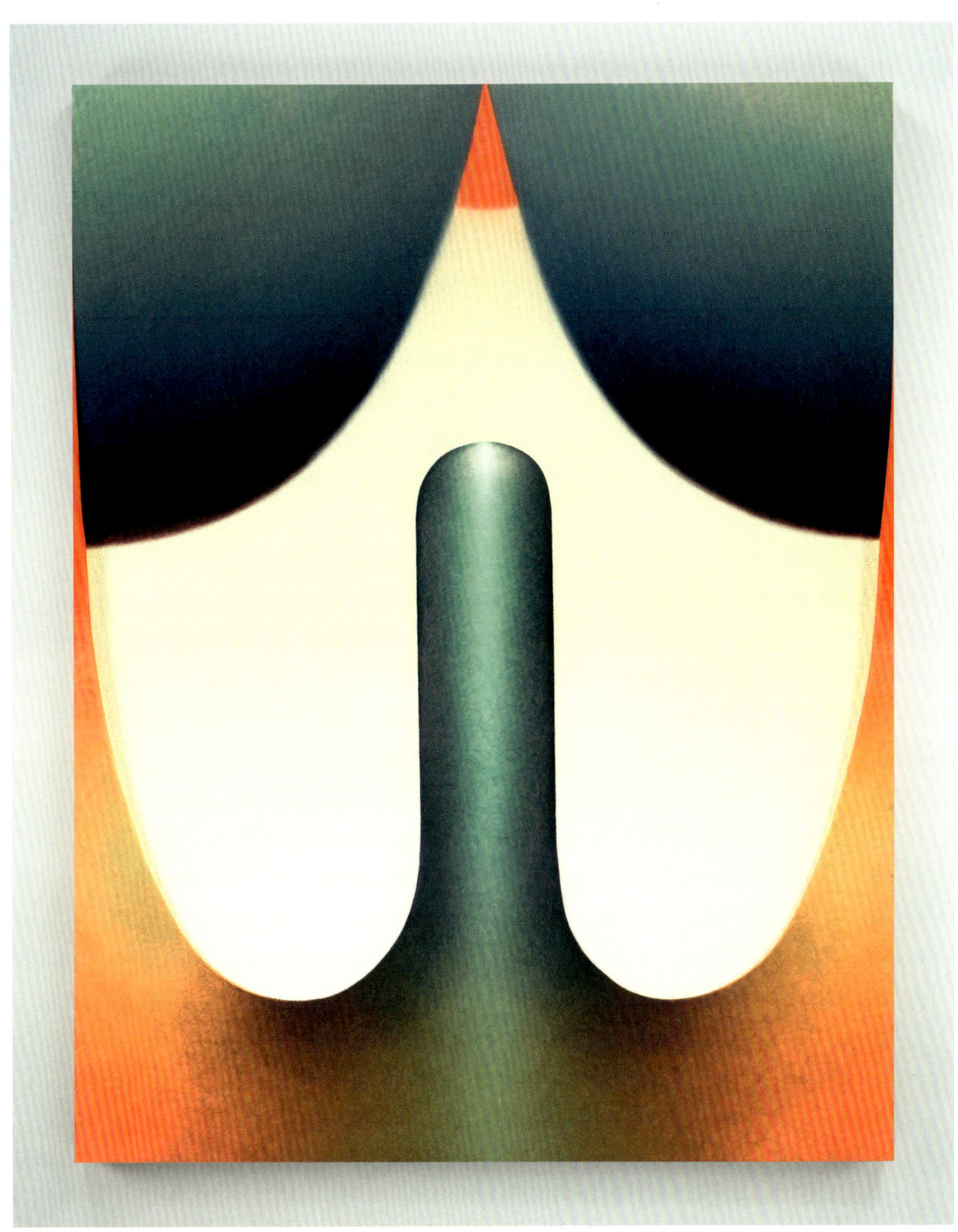

12.
Point of Entry (blue green mounds over yellow sky), 2017

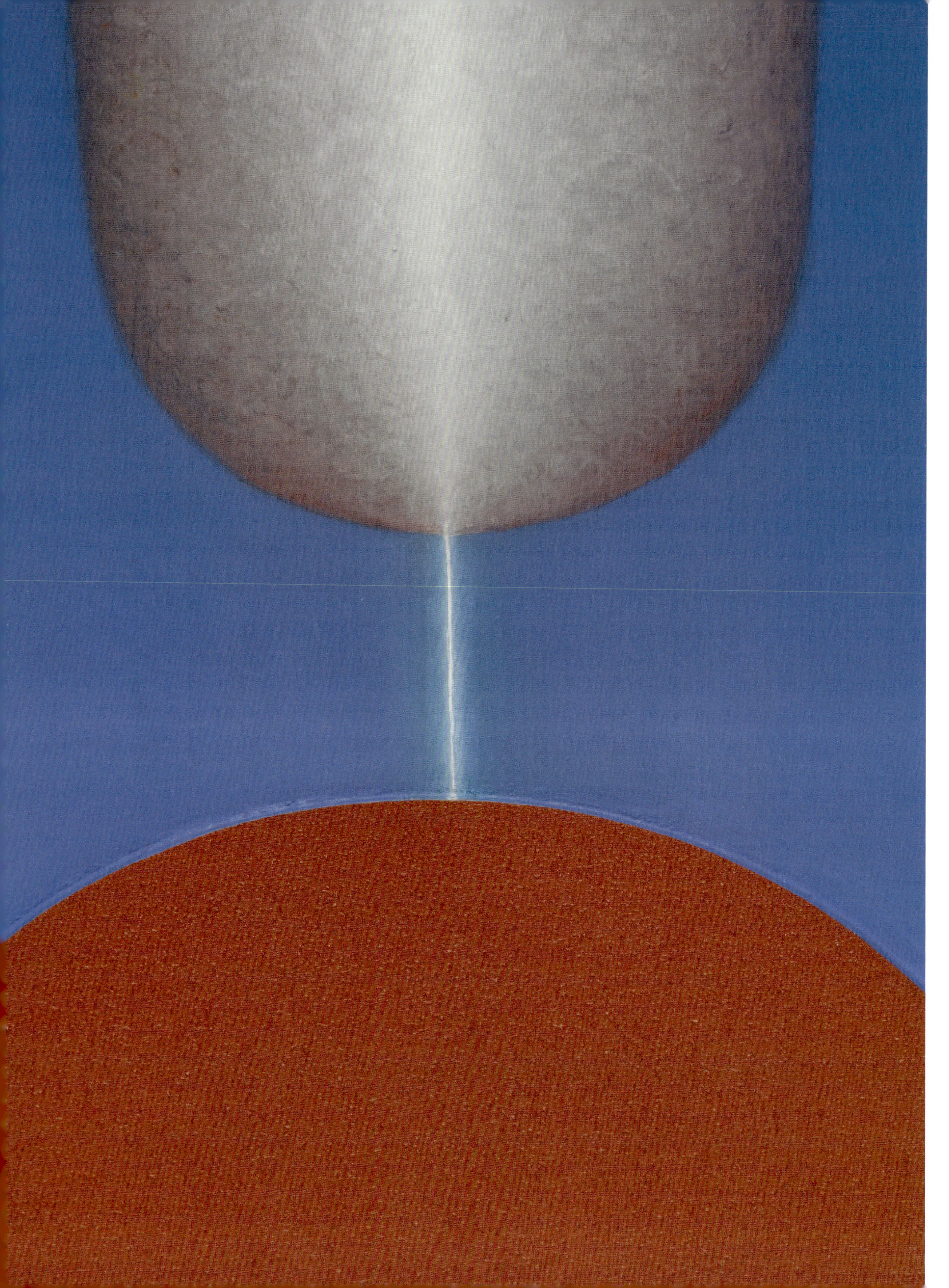

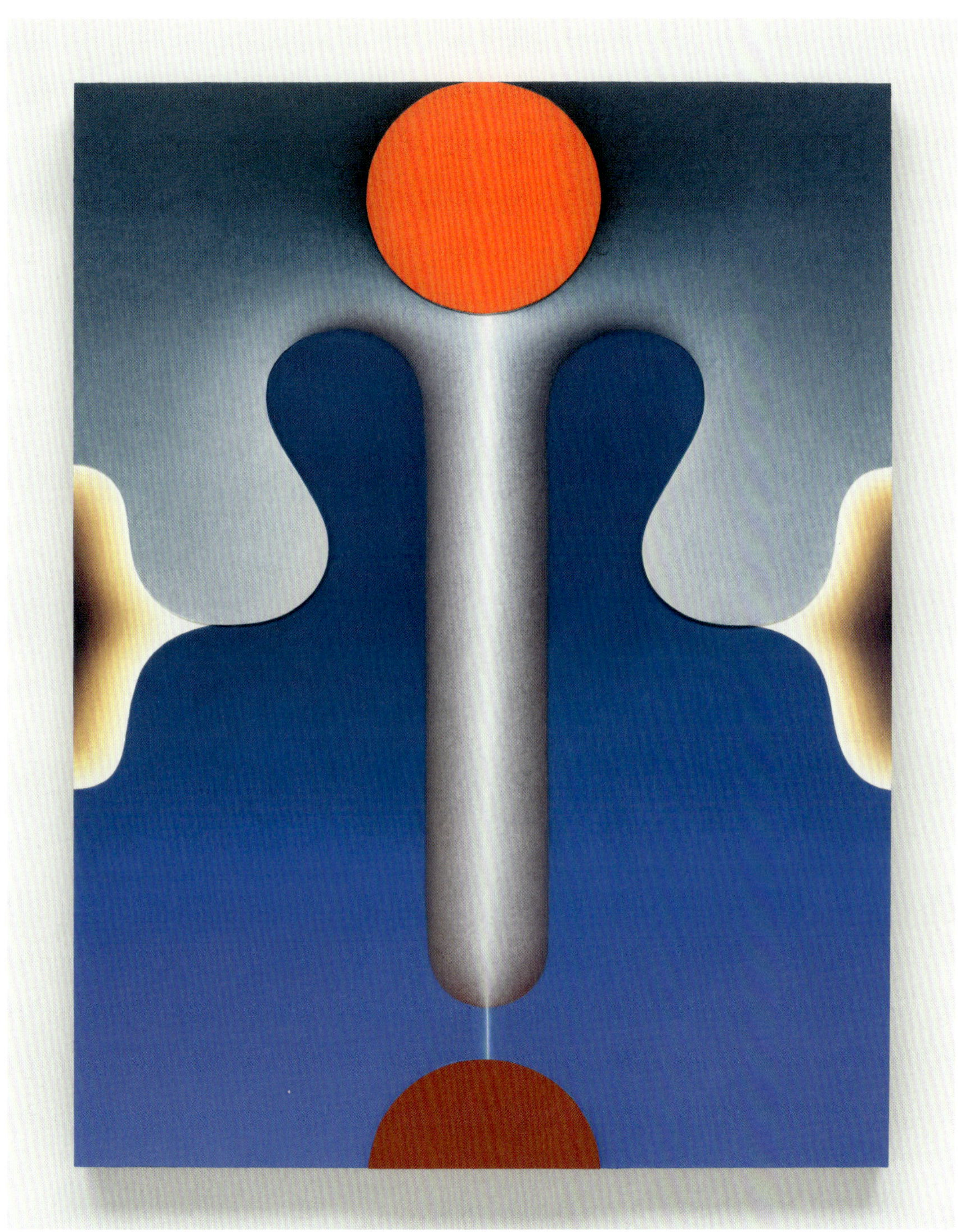

13.
Point of Entry (lingam between red circles), 2017

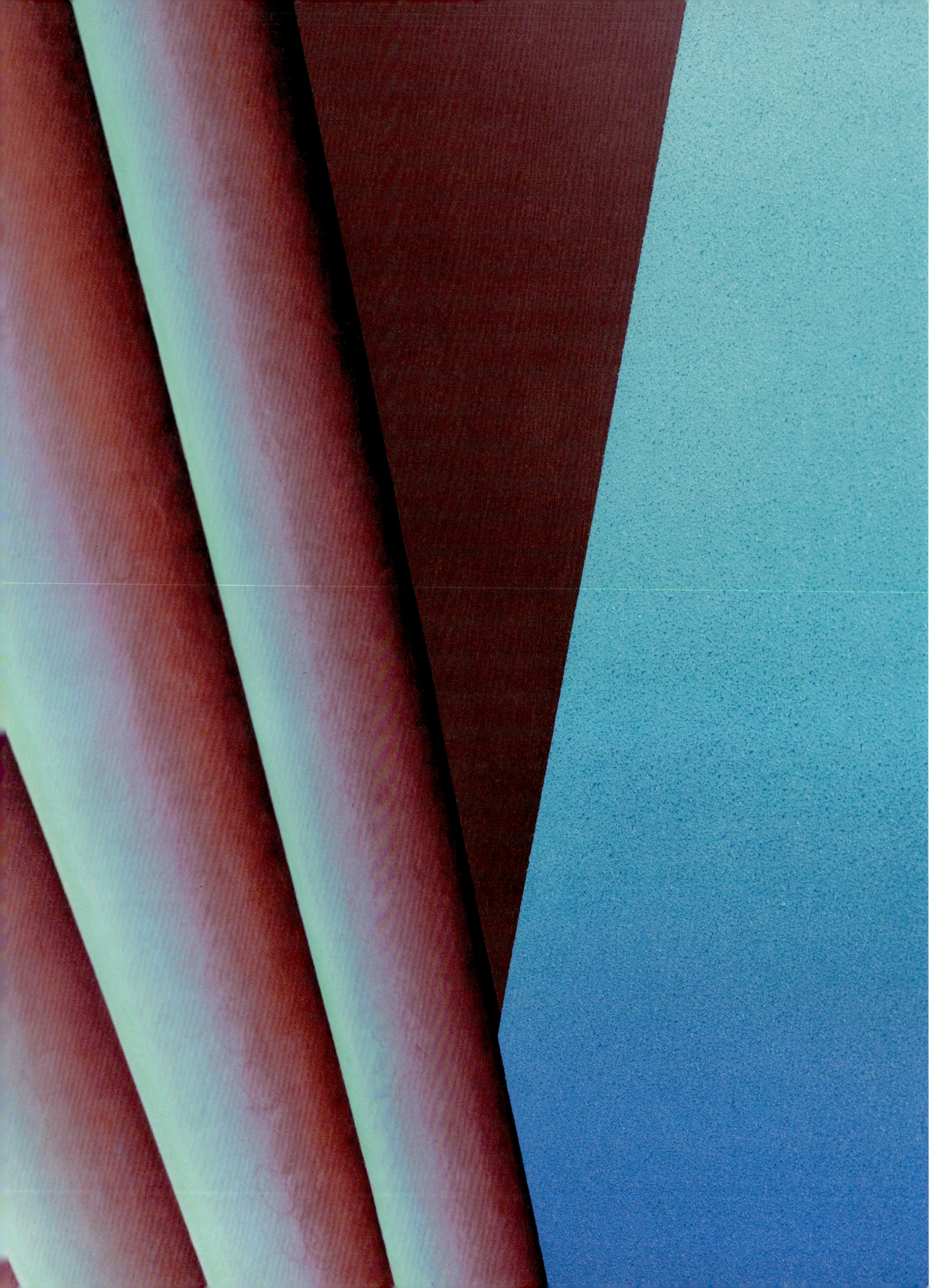

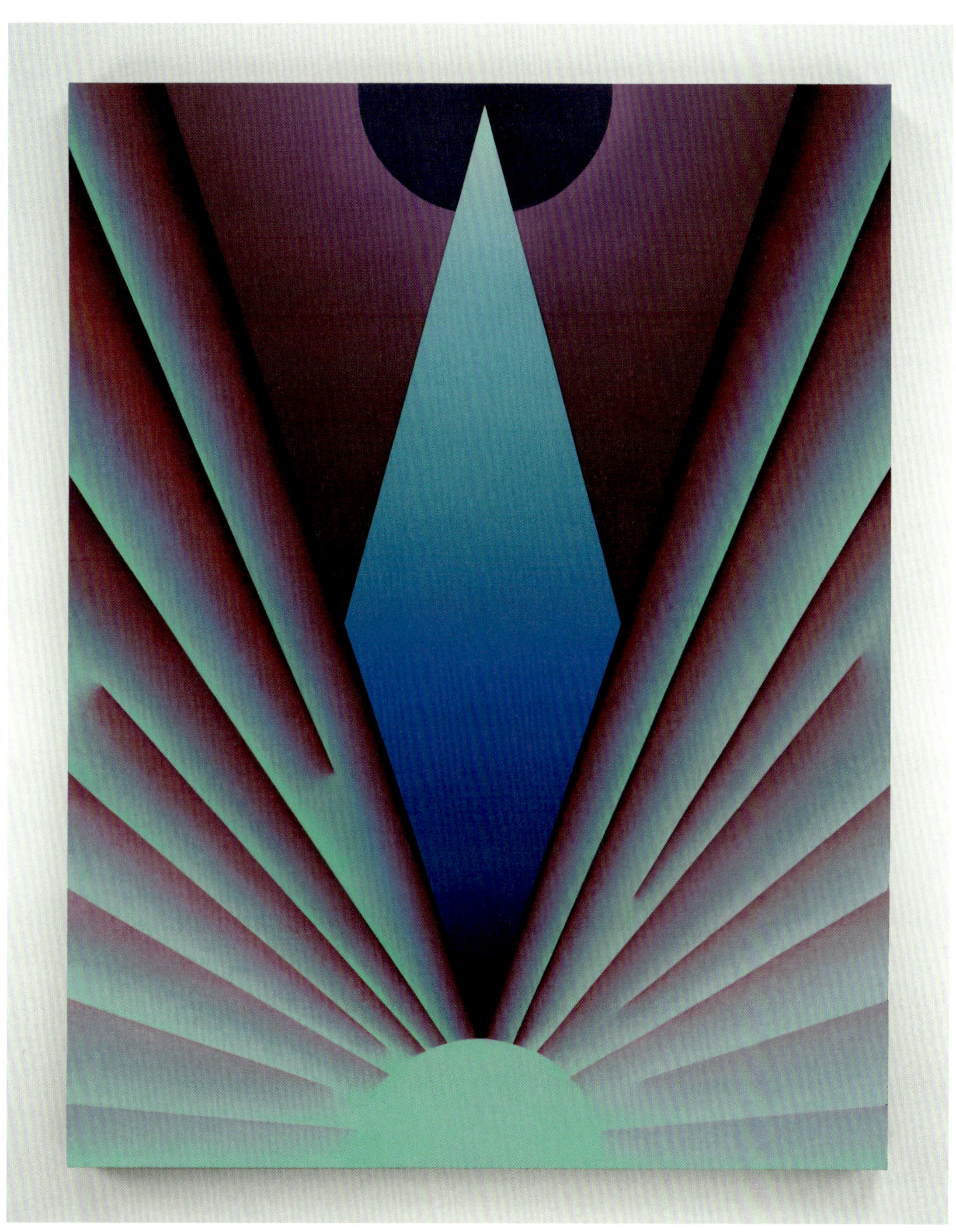

14.
The Lands Part (blue, red and purple), 2017

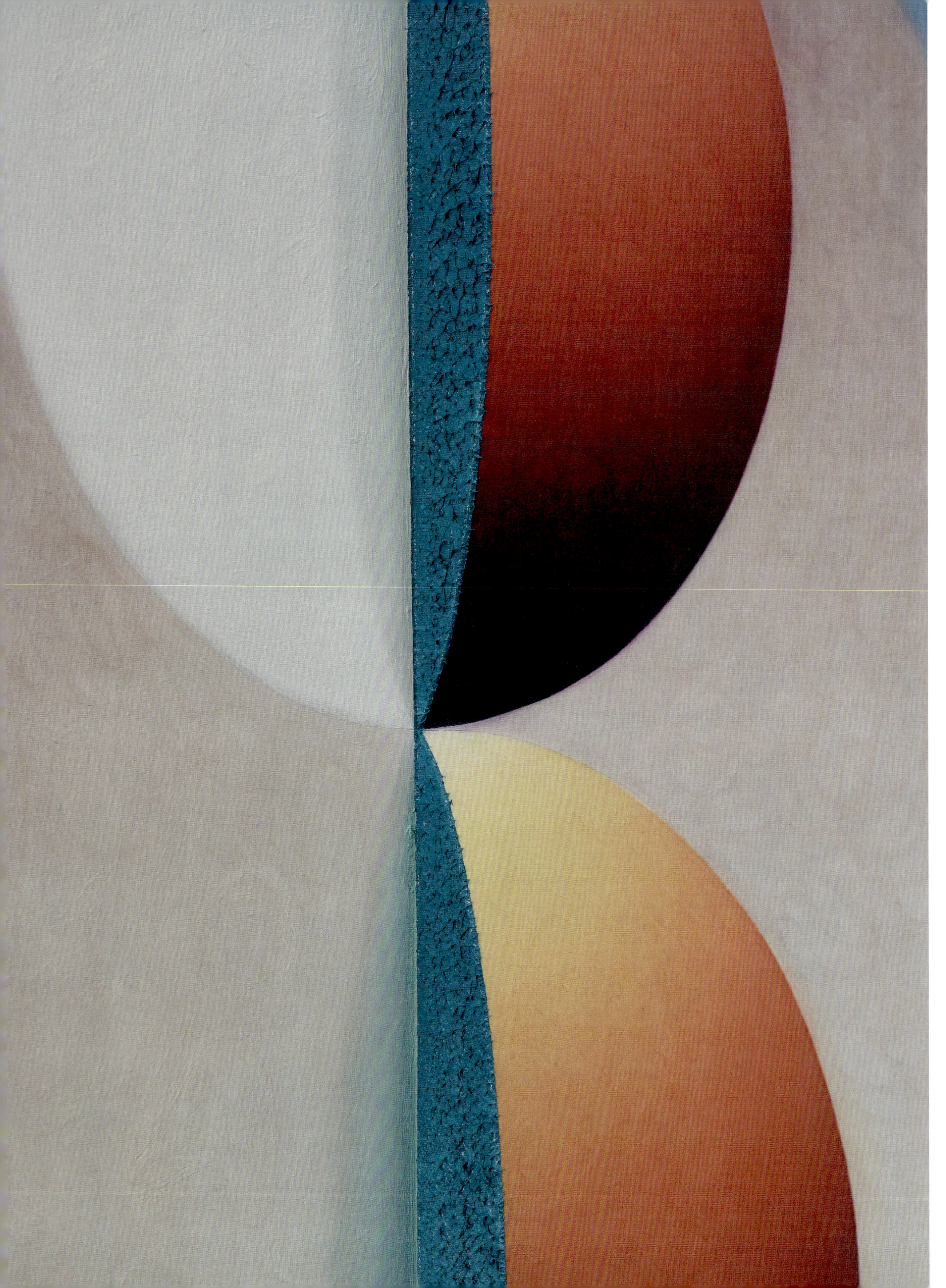

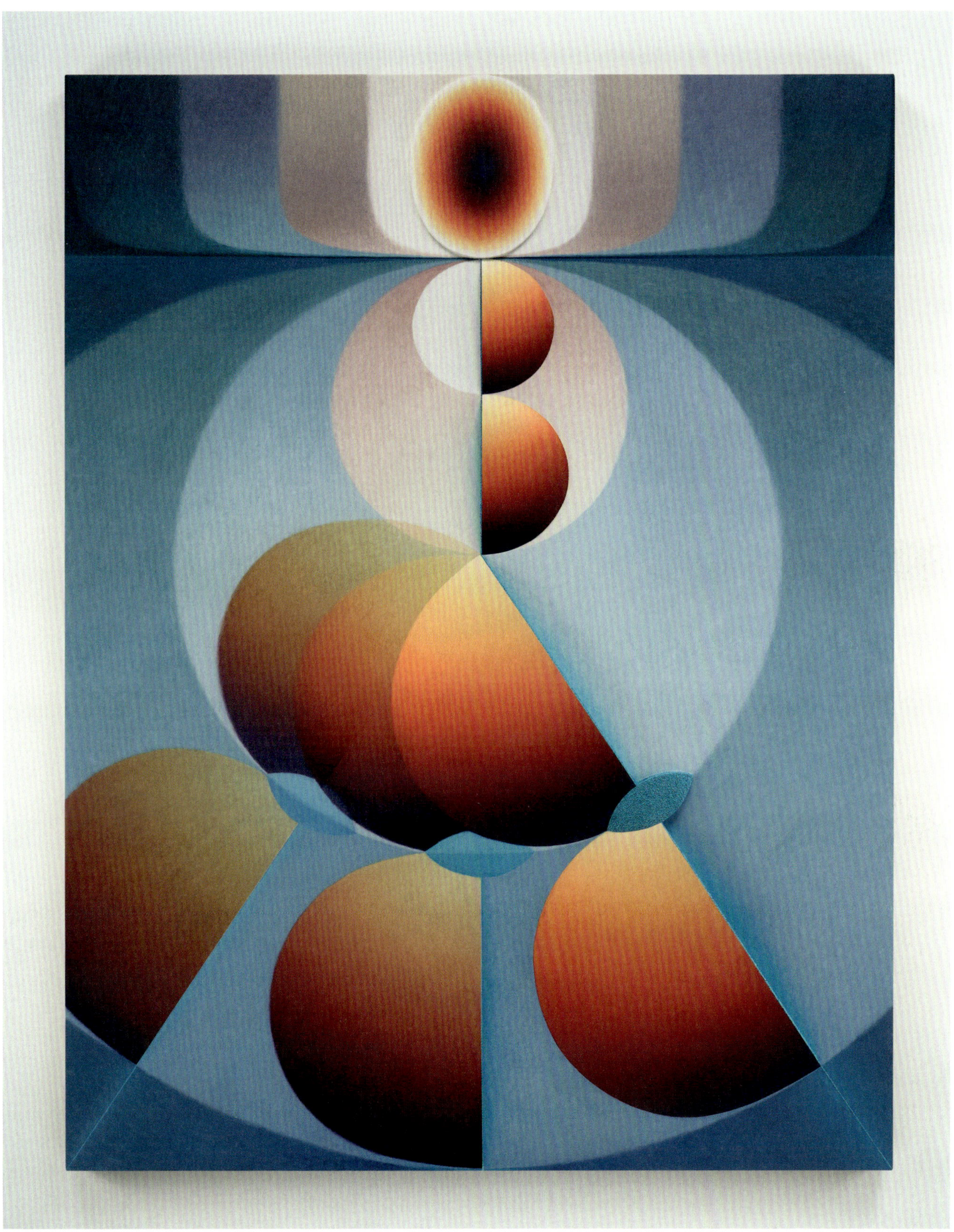

15.
Prenatal Plumb Line, 2019

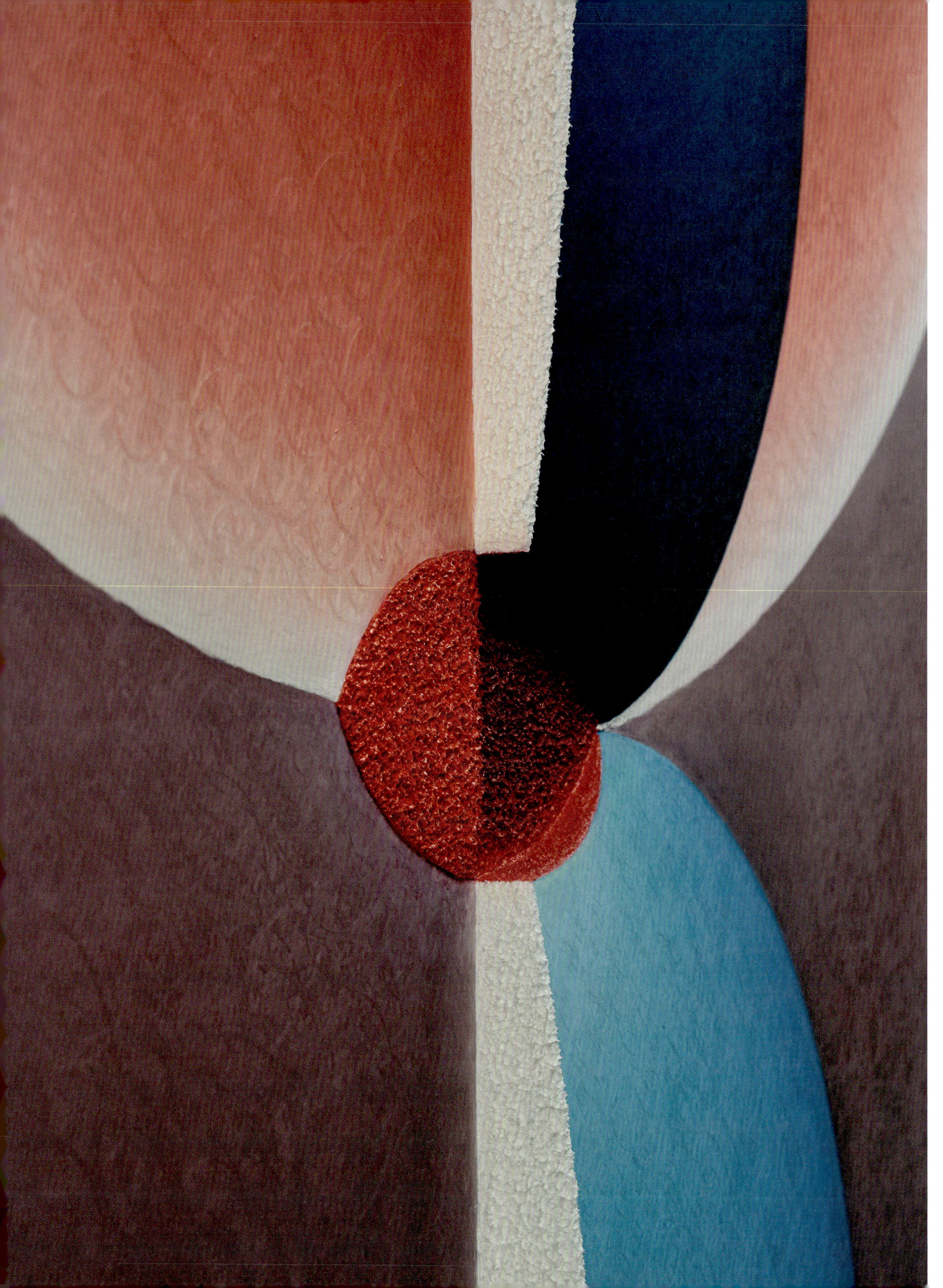

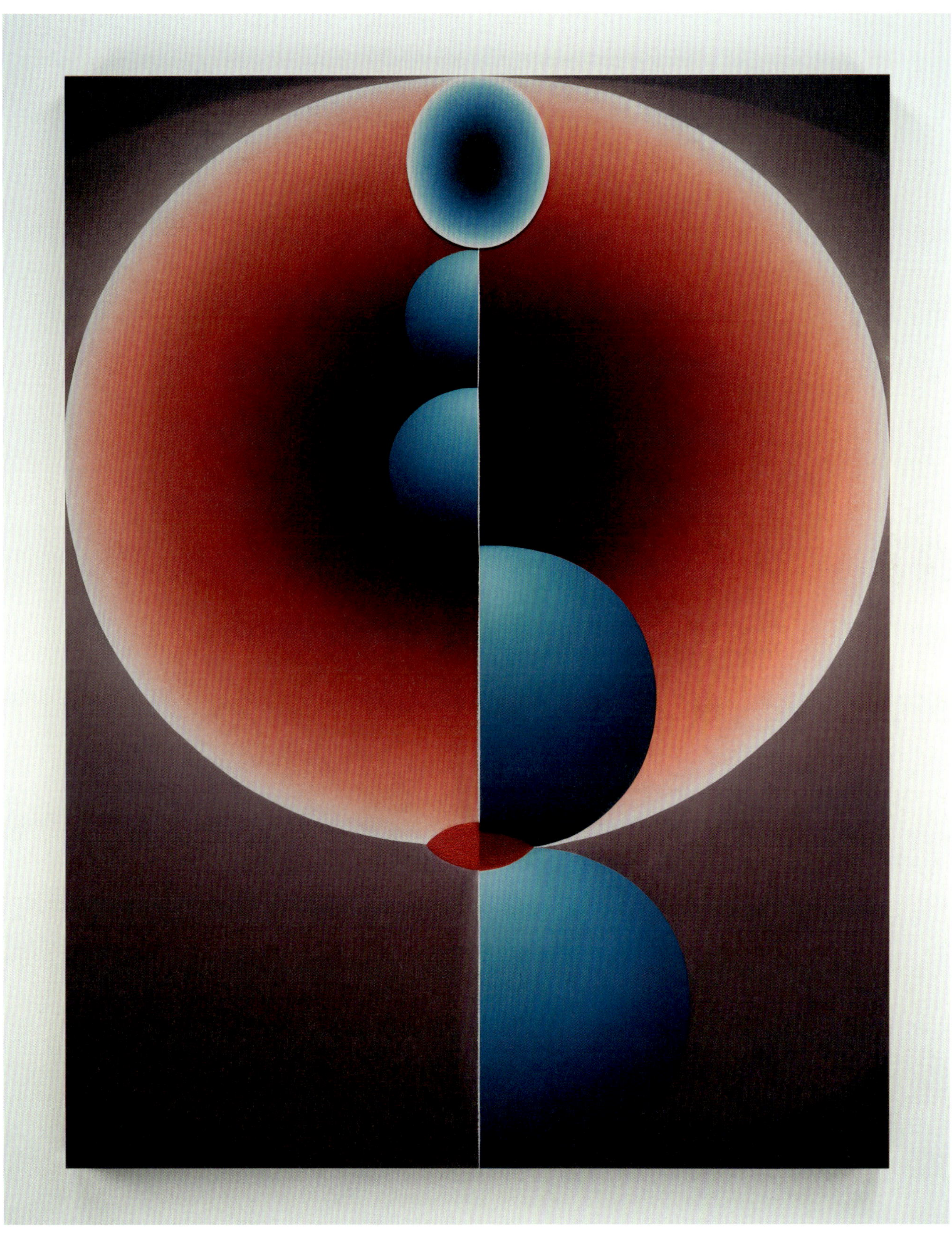

16.
Red Hole, 2019

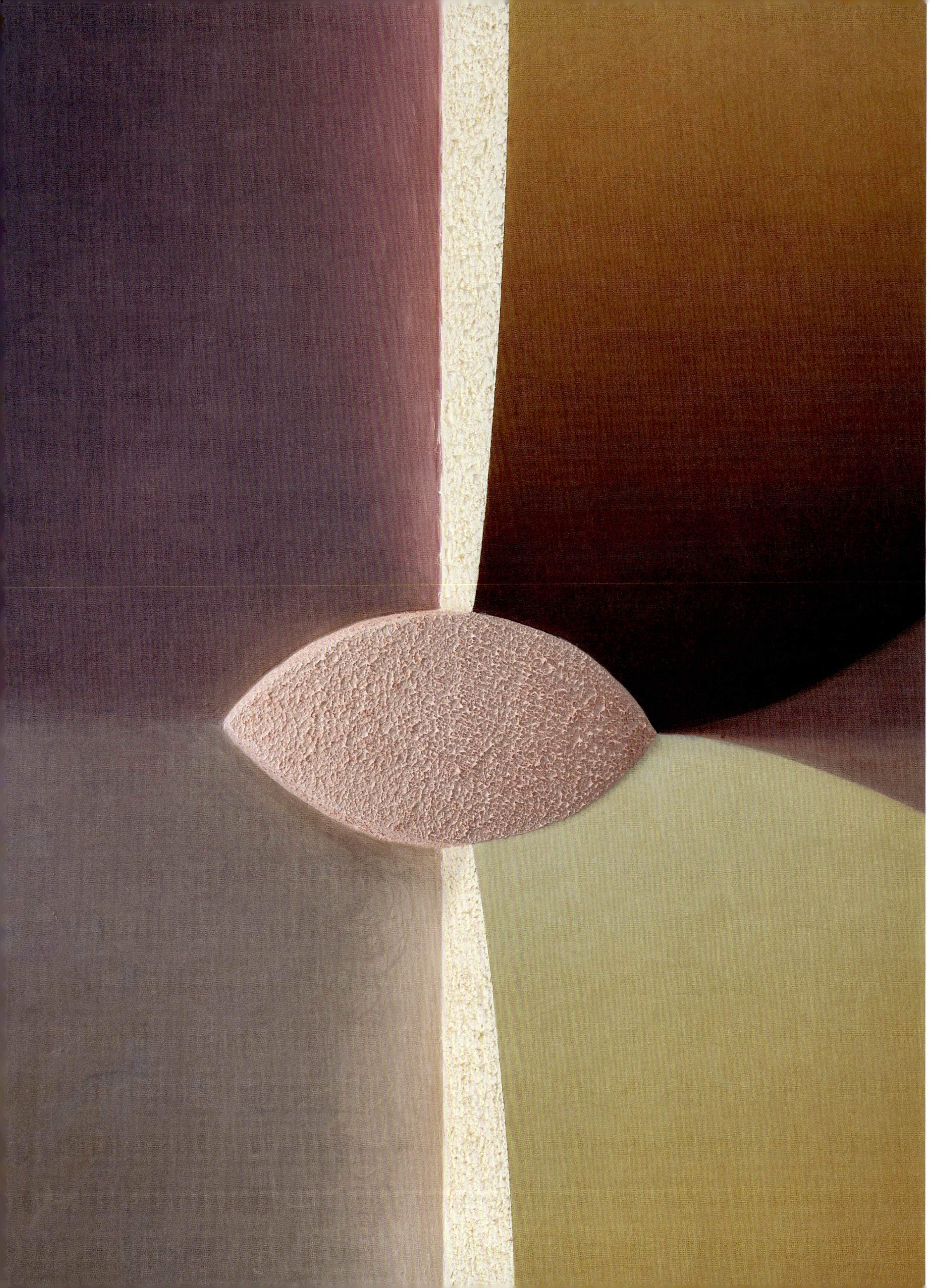

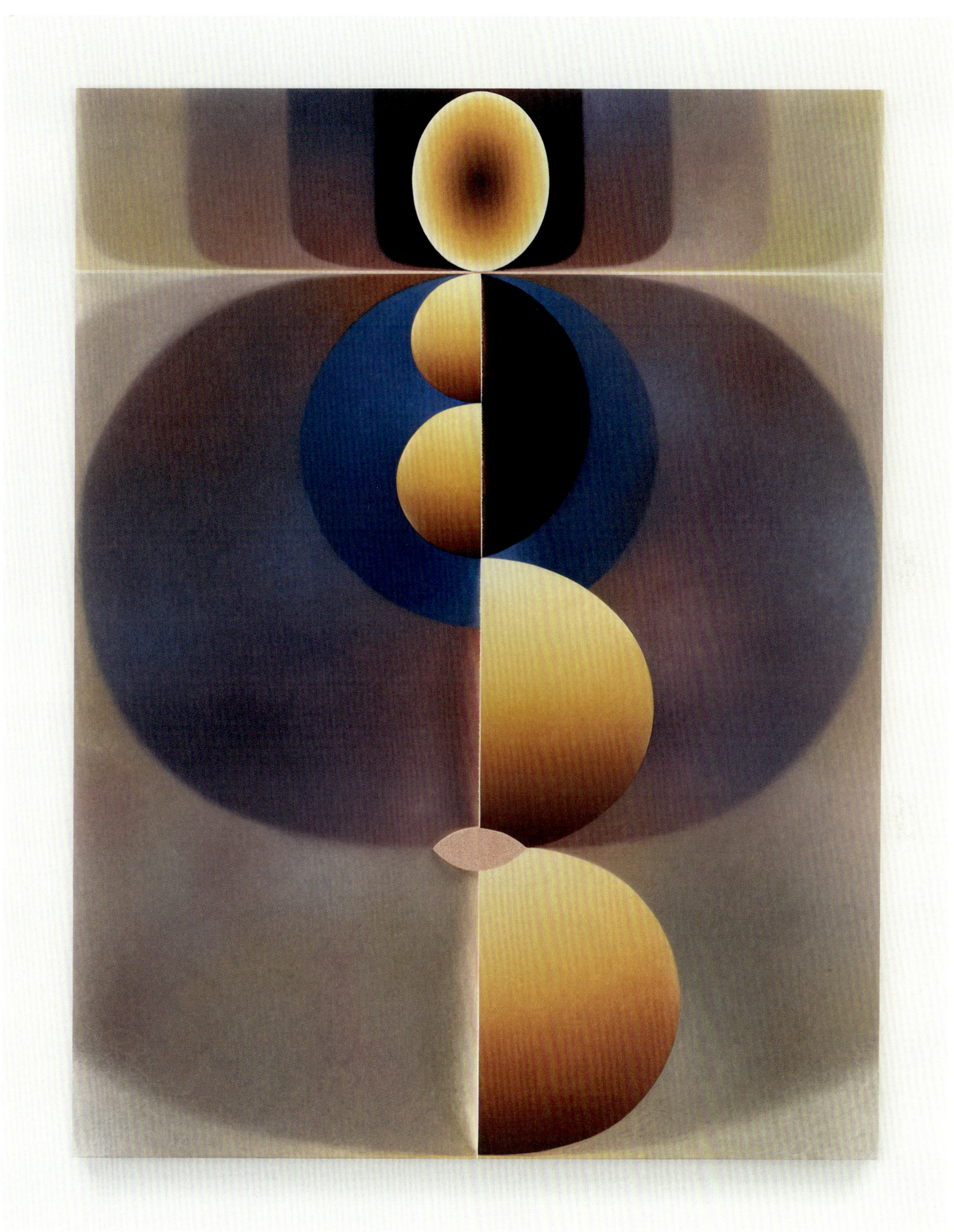

17.
Standing in yellow, pink and blue, 2019

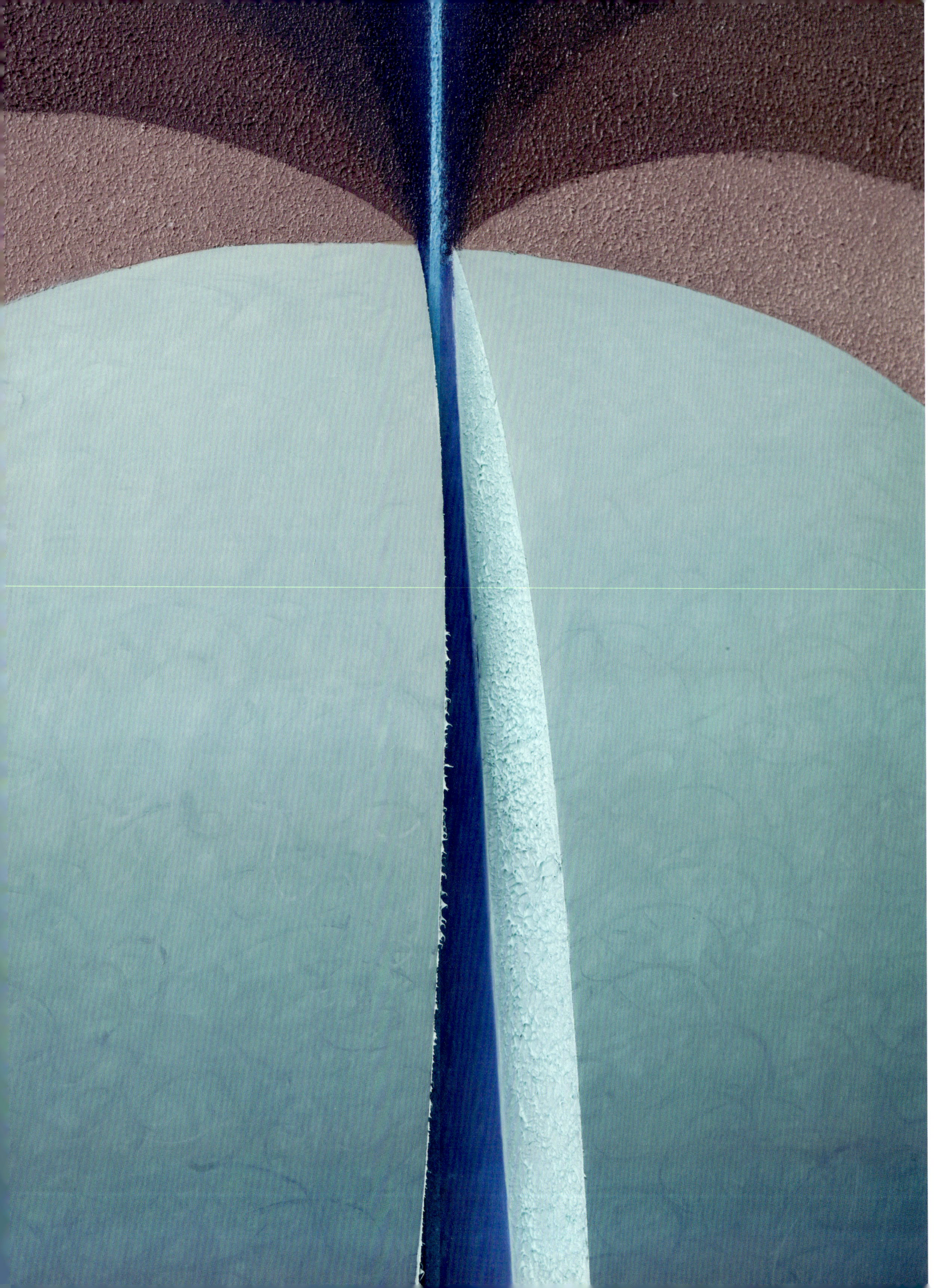

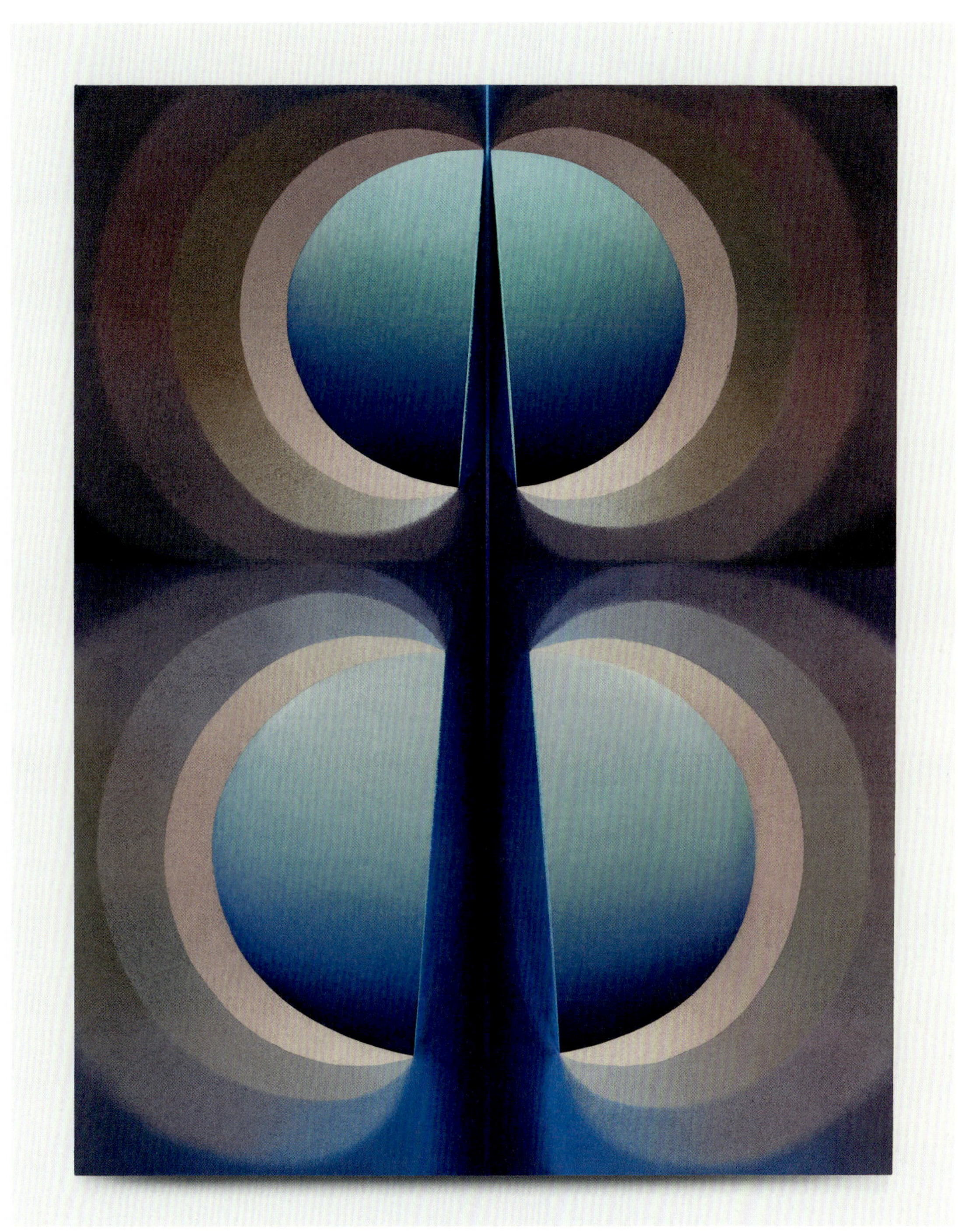

18.
Split Orbs in teal and mauve, 2021

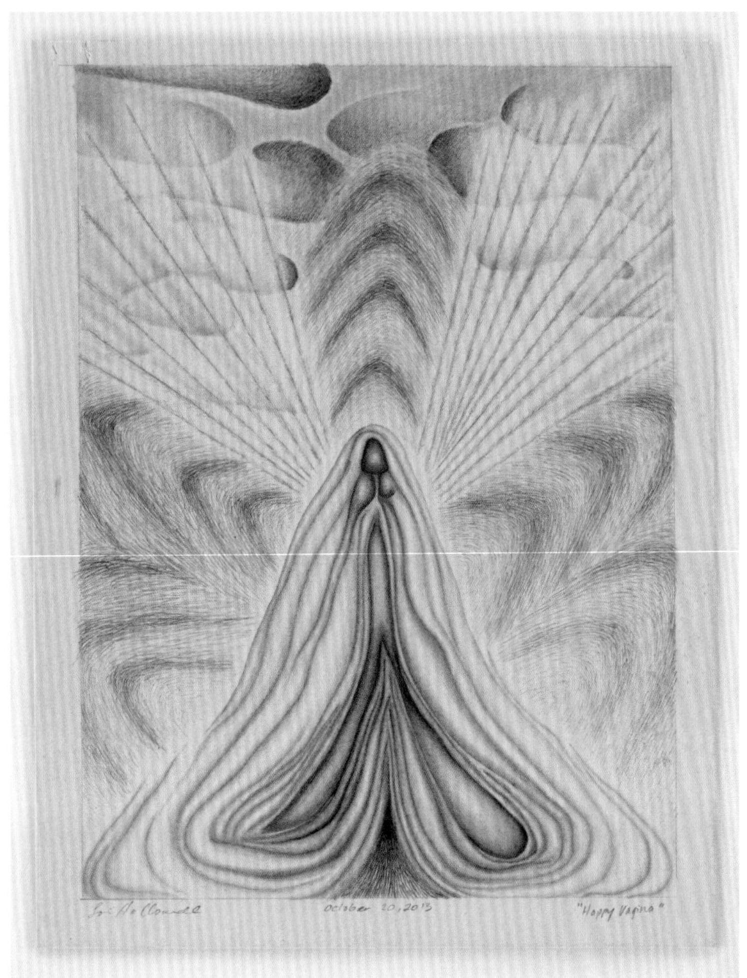

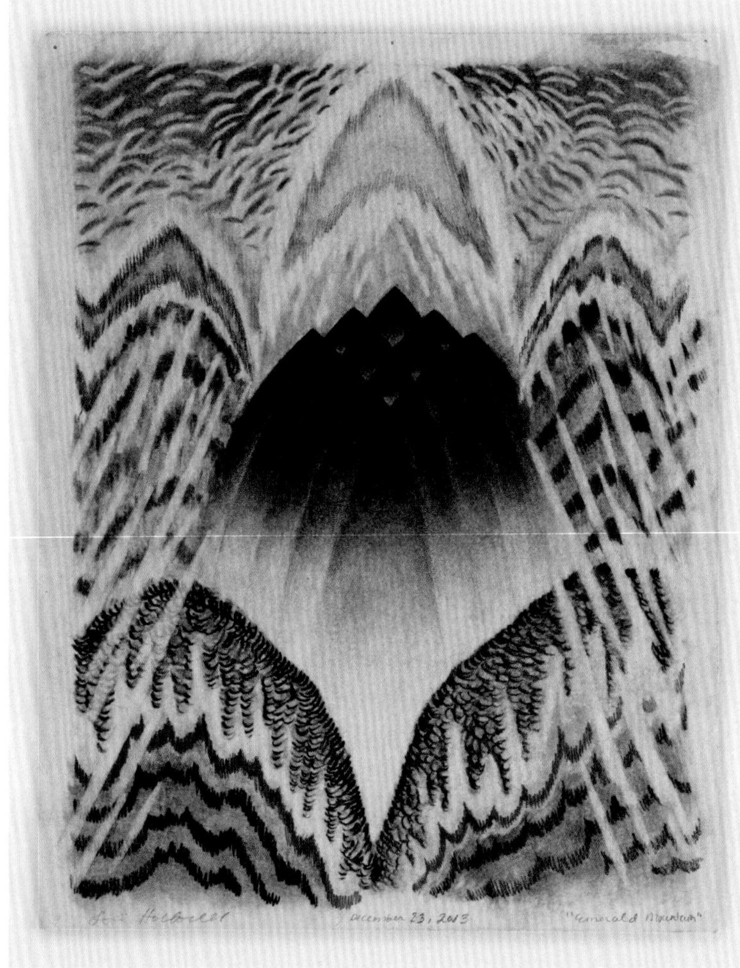

19.
Happy Vagina
October 20, 2013

20.
Emerald Mountain
December 23, 2013

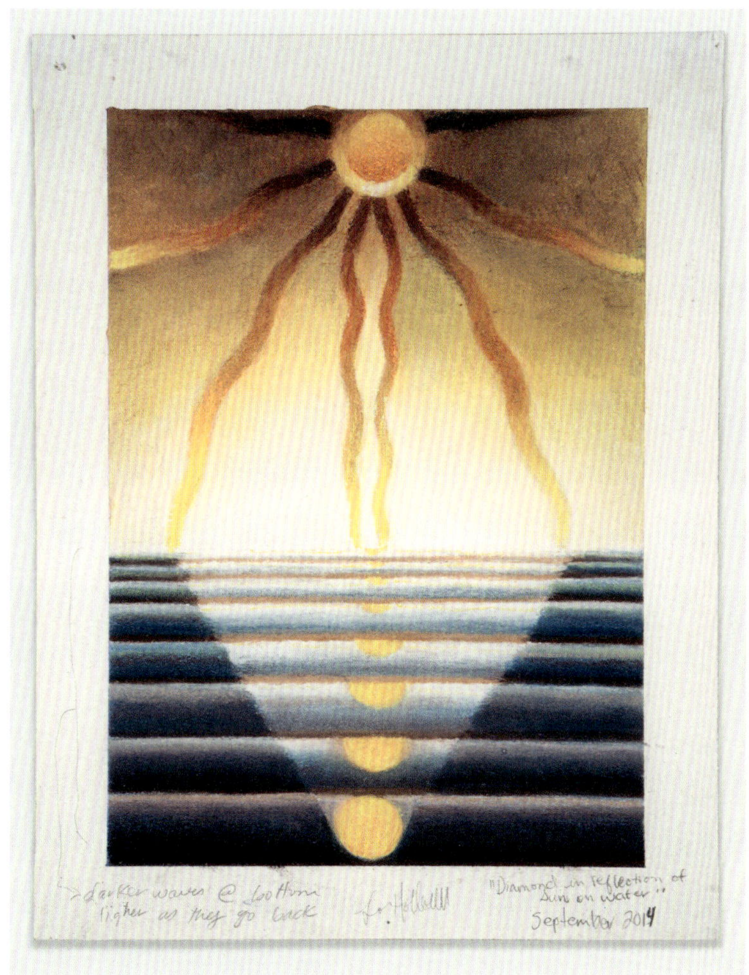

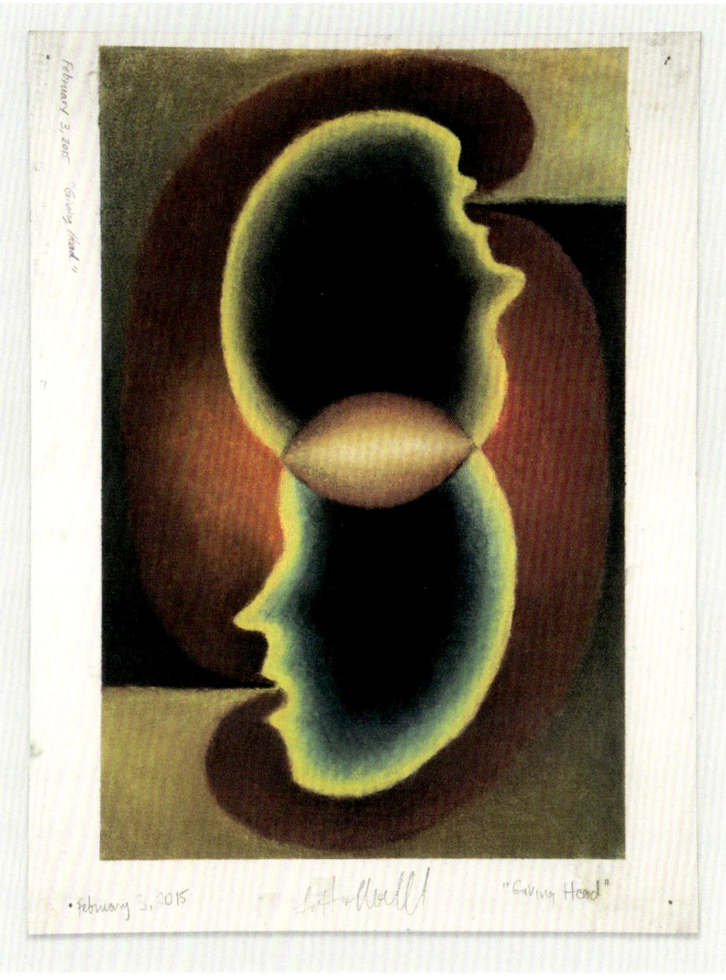

21.
Diamond in reflection of sun on water
September 2014

22.
Giving Head
February 3, 2015

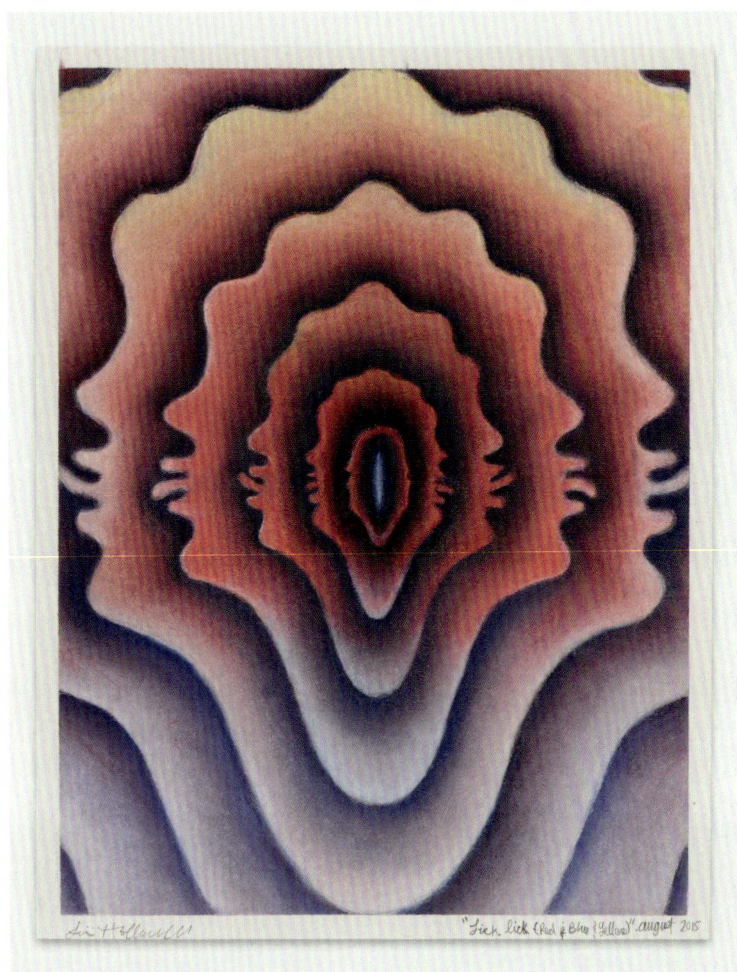

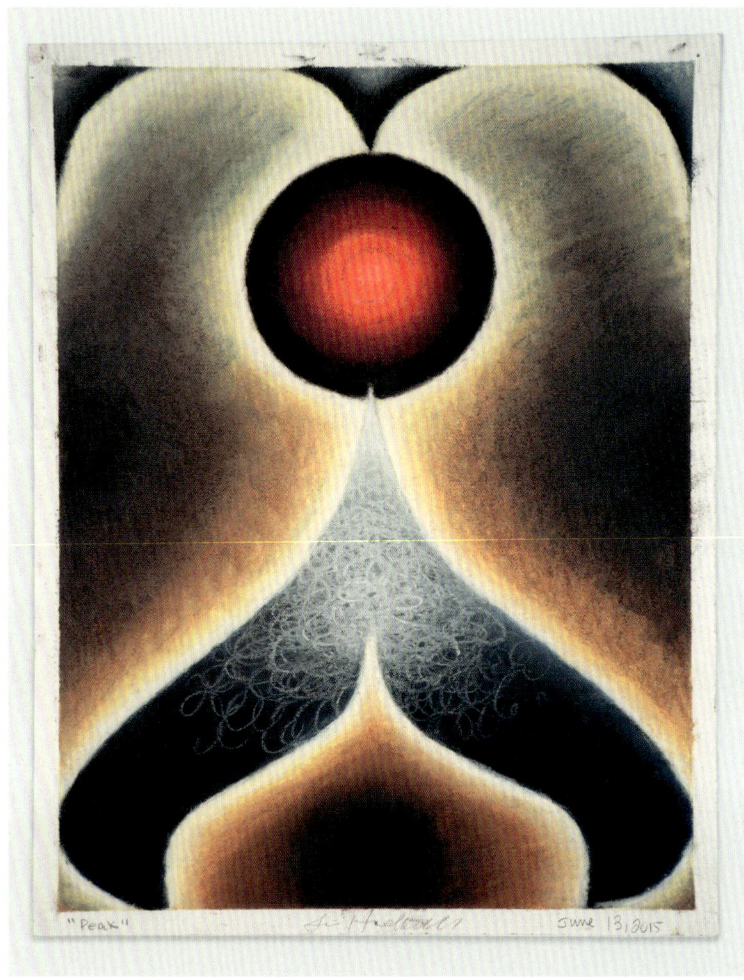

23.
Lick Lick (Red & Blue & Yellow)
August 2015

24.
Peak
June 13, 2015

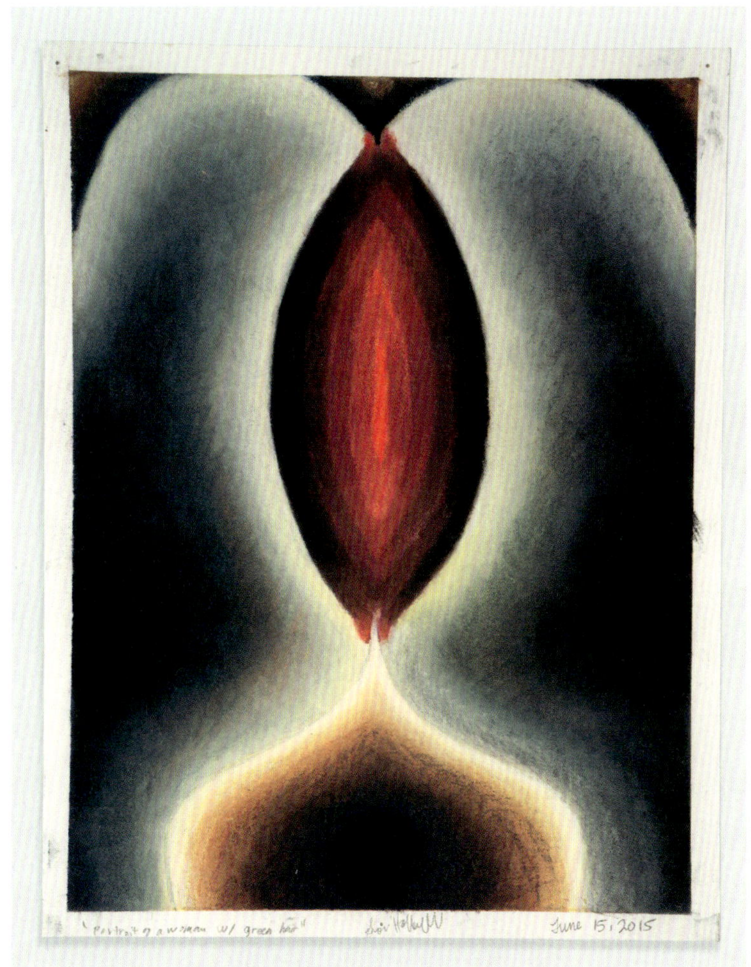

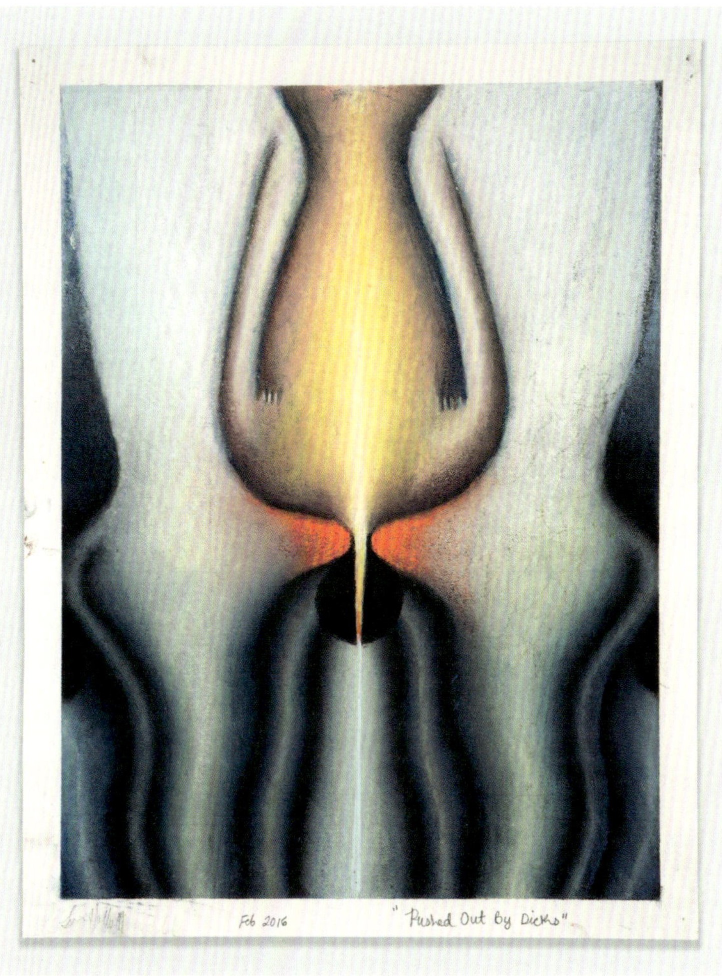

25.
Portrait of a woman with green hair
June 15, 2015

26.
Pushed out by dicks
February 2016

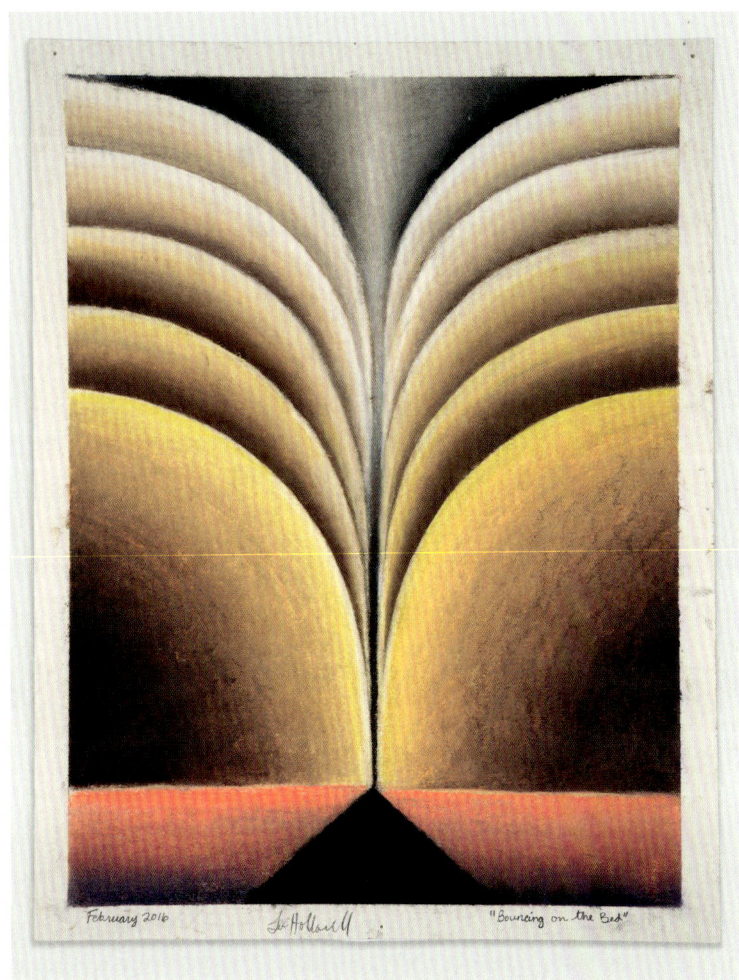

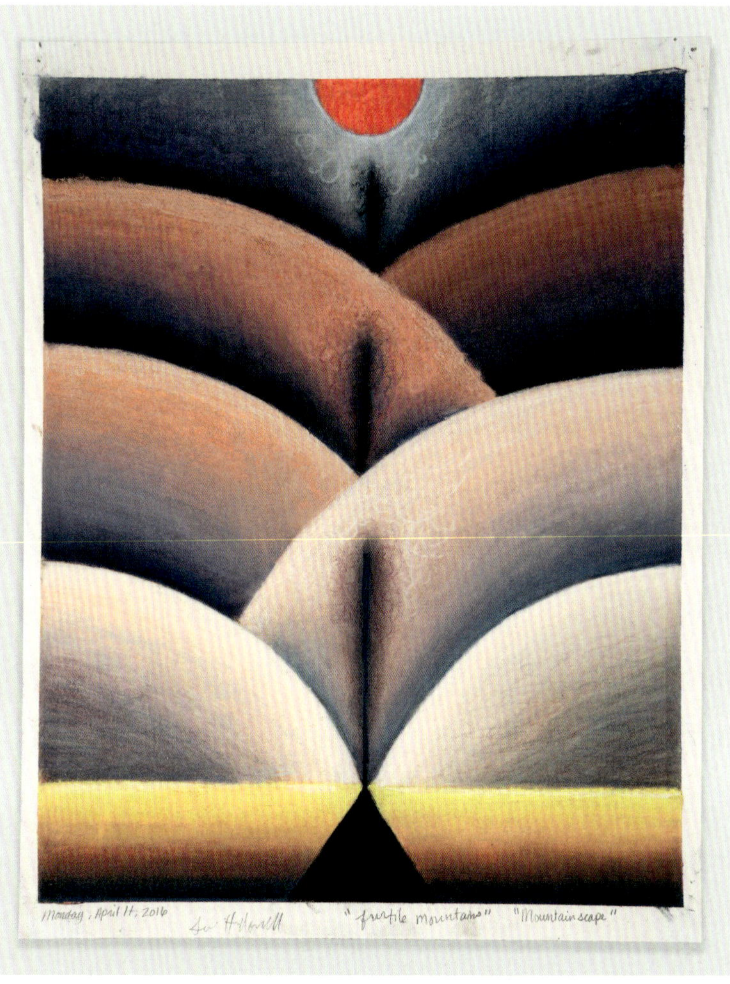

27.
Bouncing on the Bed
February 2016

28.
Mountainscape
April 11, 2016

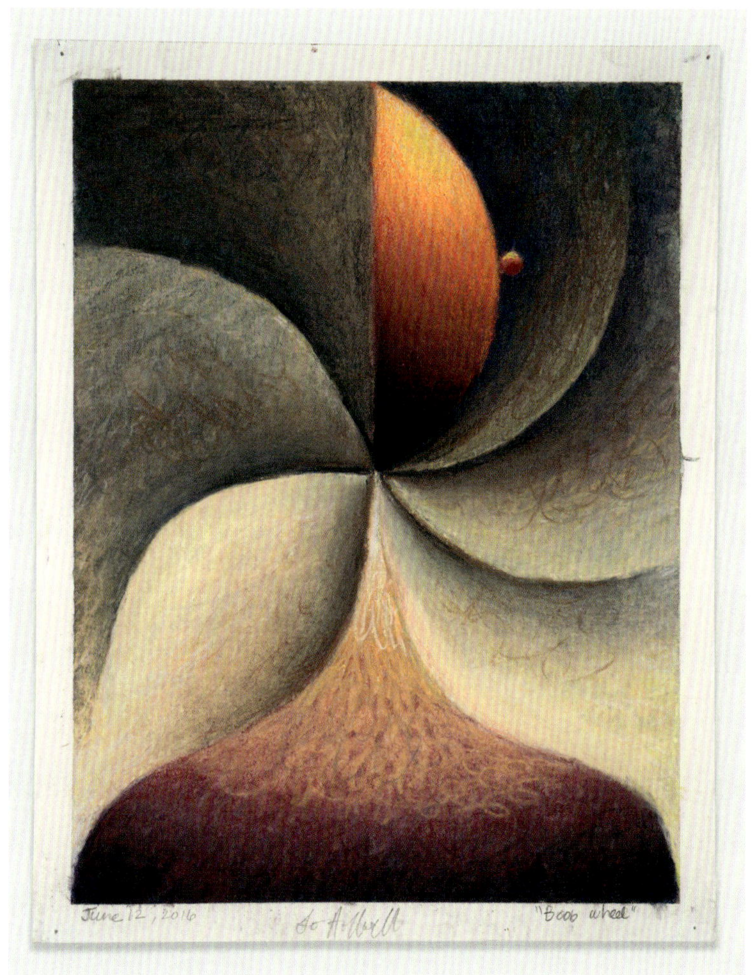

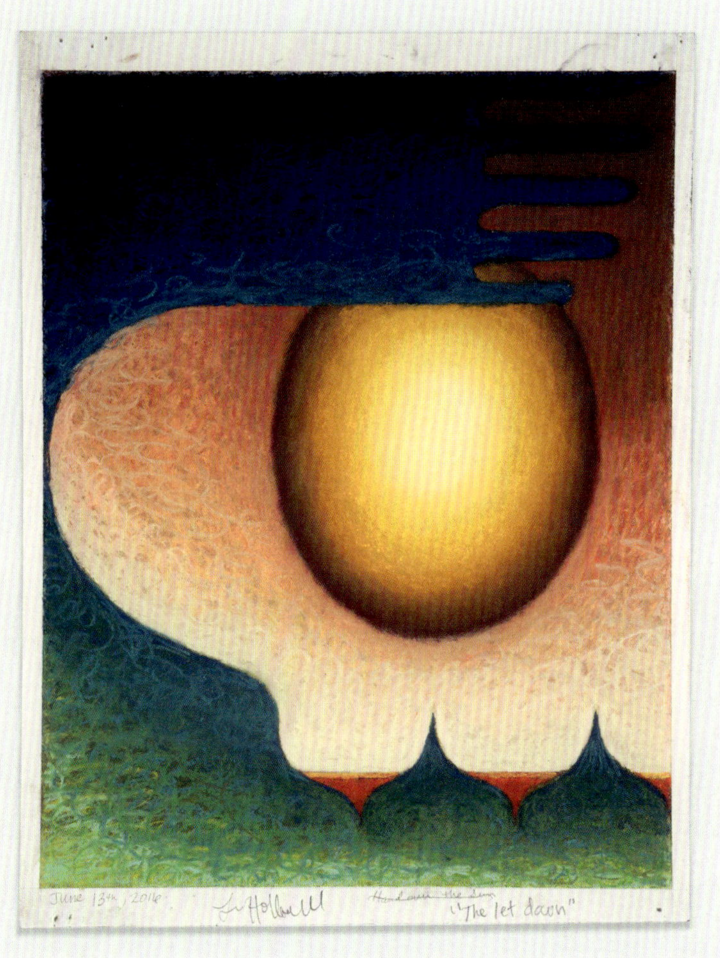

29.
Boob Wheel
June 12, 2016

30.
The Let Down
June 13, 2016

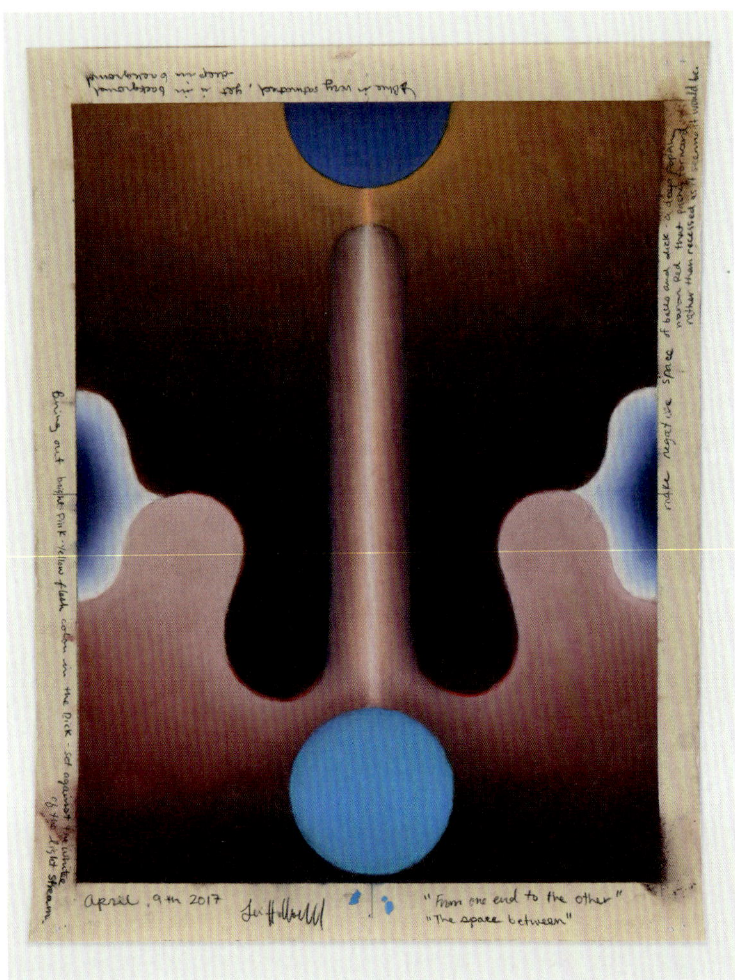

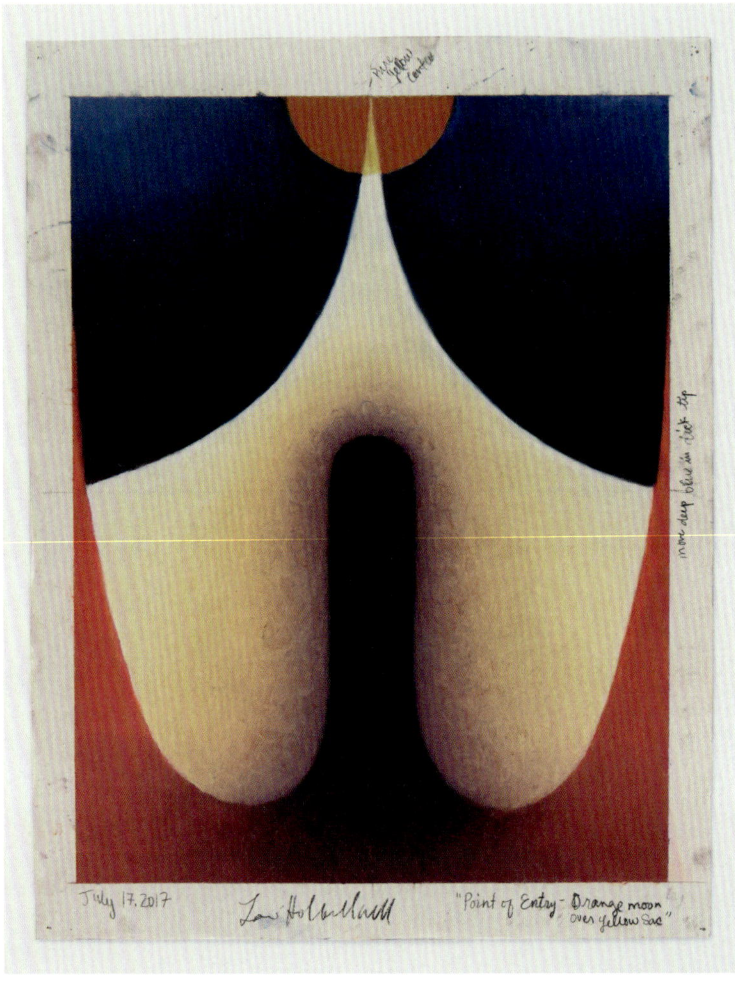

31.
Space Between (from one end to the other)
April 9, 2017

32.
Point of Entry (orange moon over yellow sac)
July 17, 2017

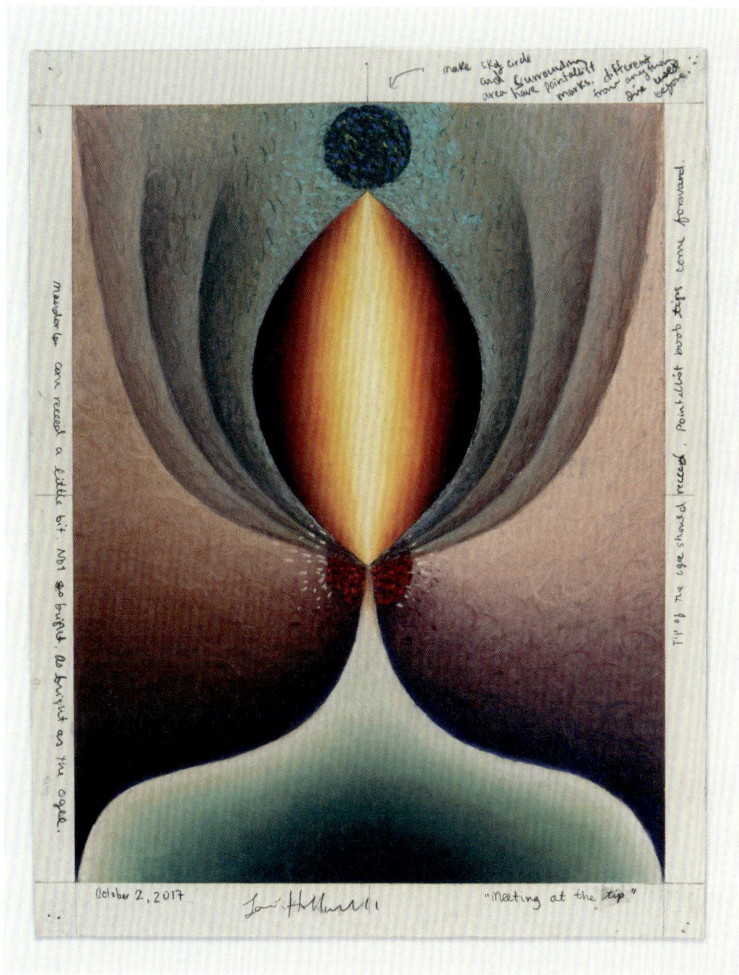

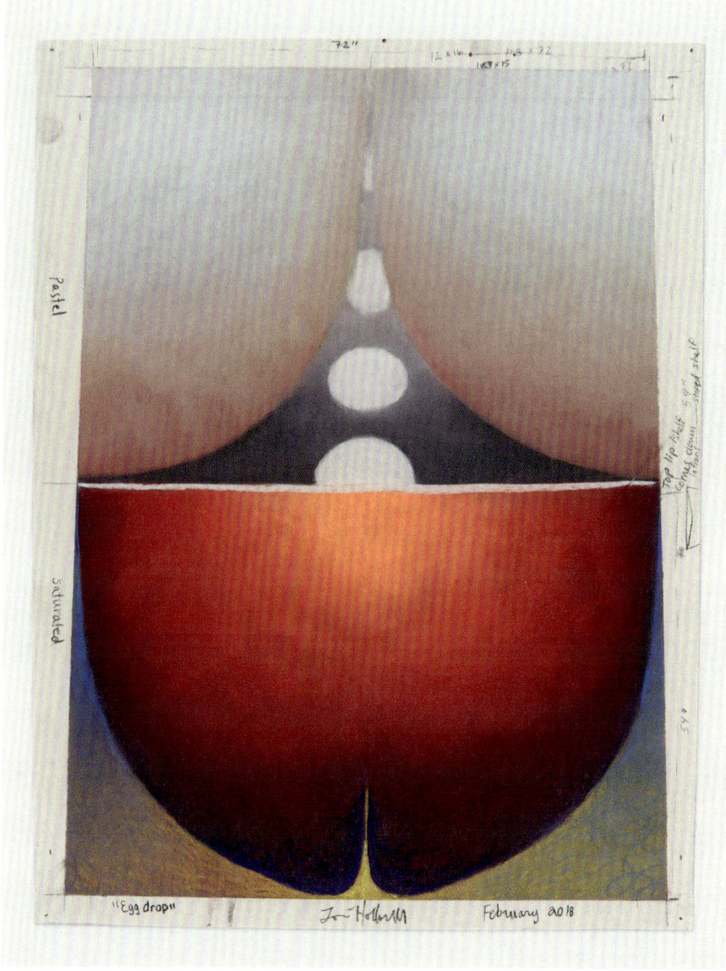

33.
Meeting at the Tip
October 2, 2017

34.
Egg Drop
February 2018

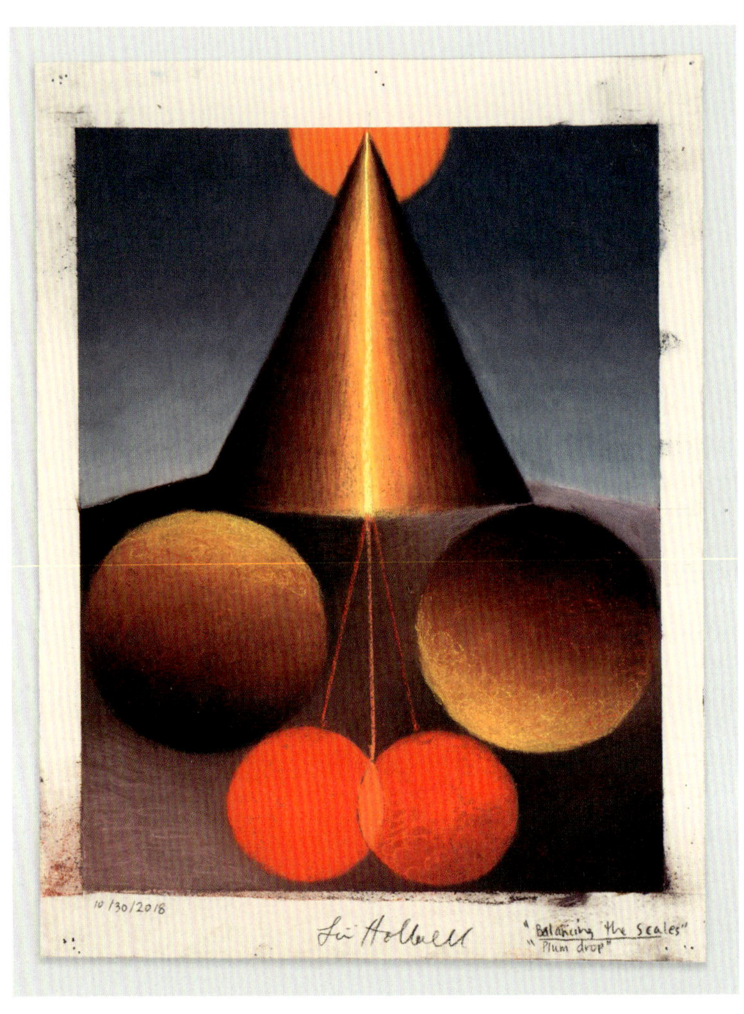

35.
Balancing the scale
October 30, 2018

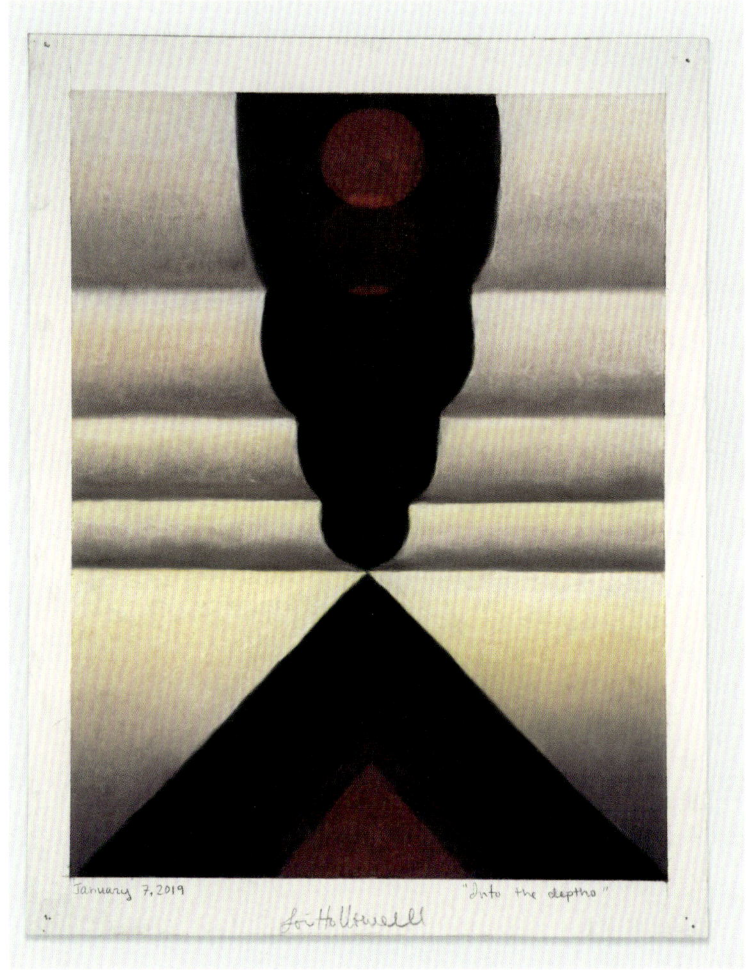

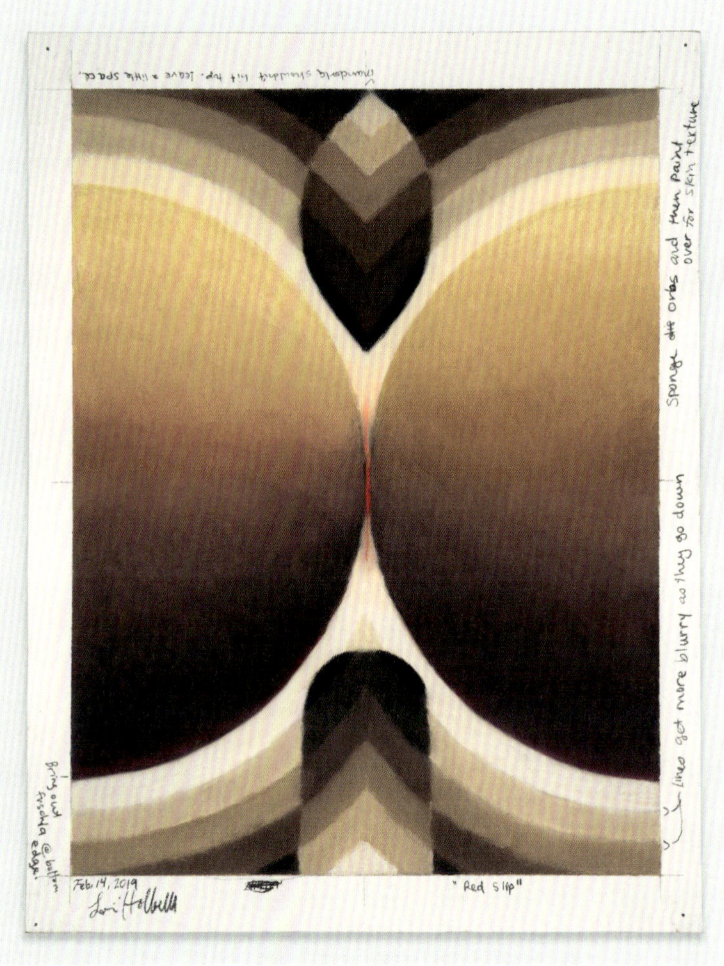

36.
Into the depths
January 7, 2019

37.
Red Slip
February 14, 2019

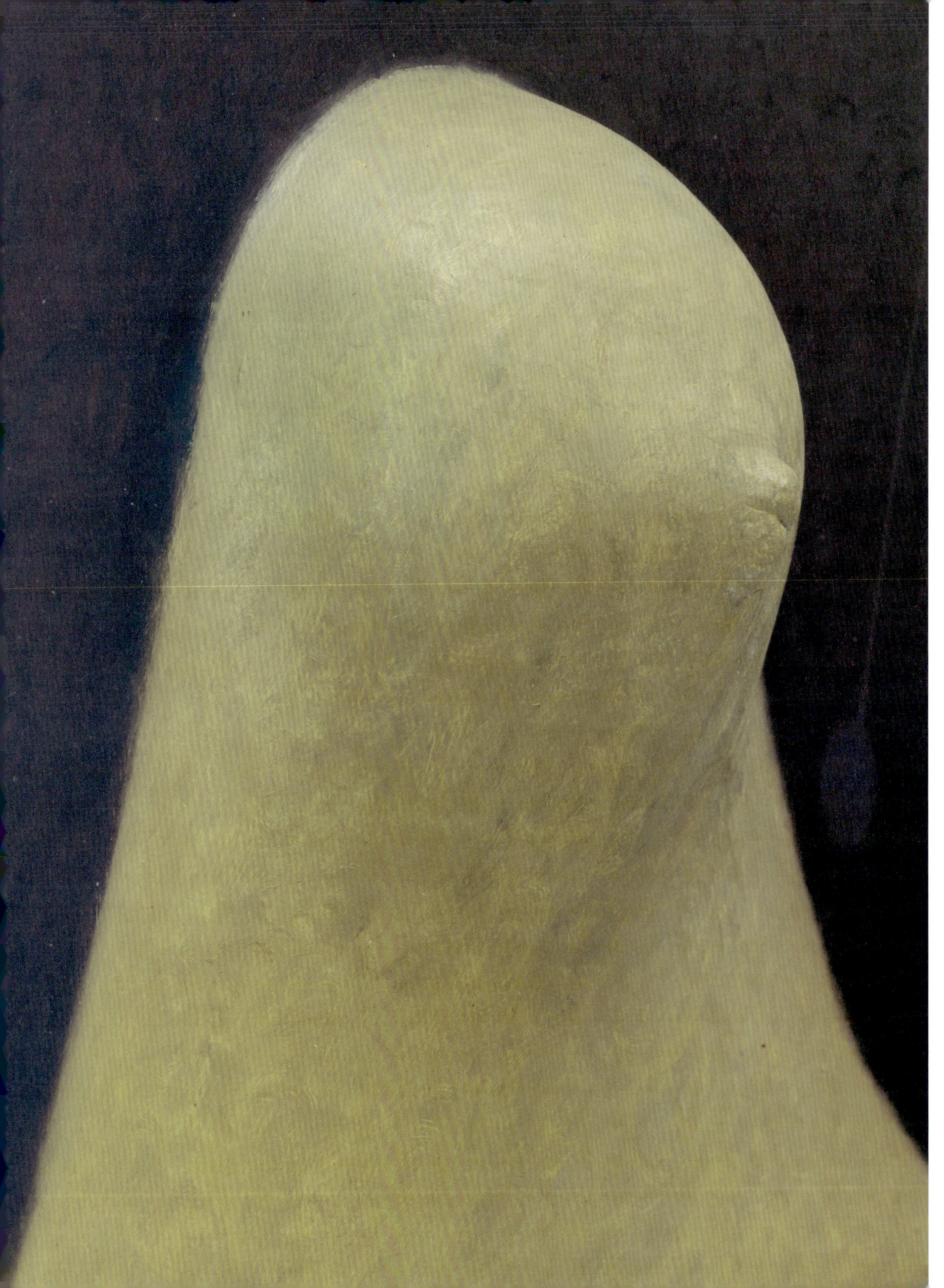

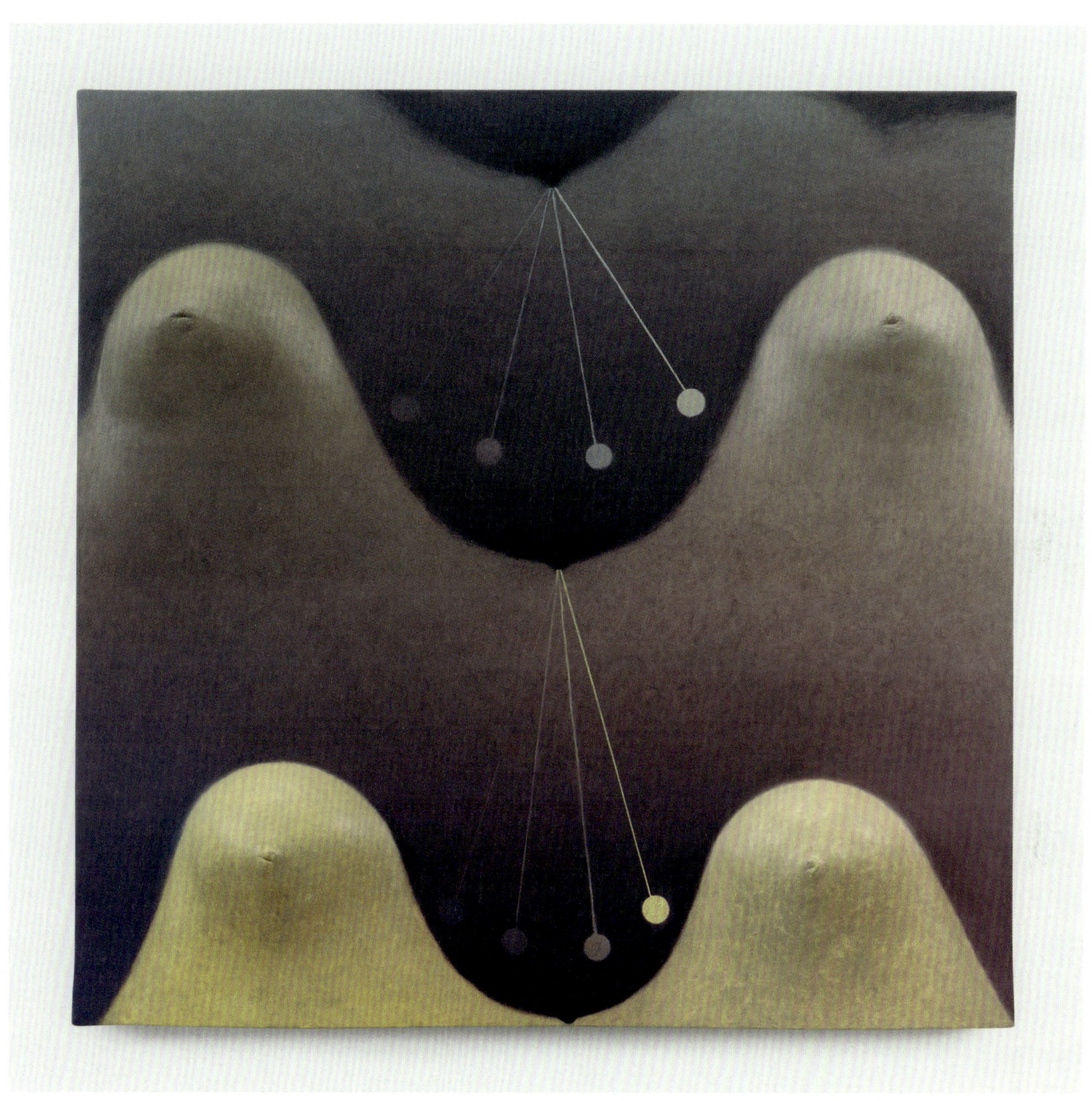

38.
Tick-Tock Belly Clock, 2021

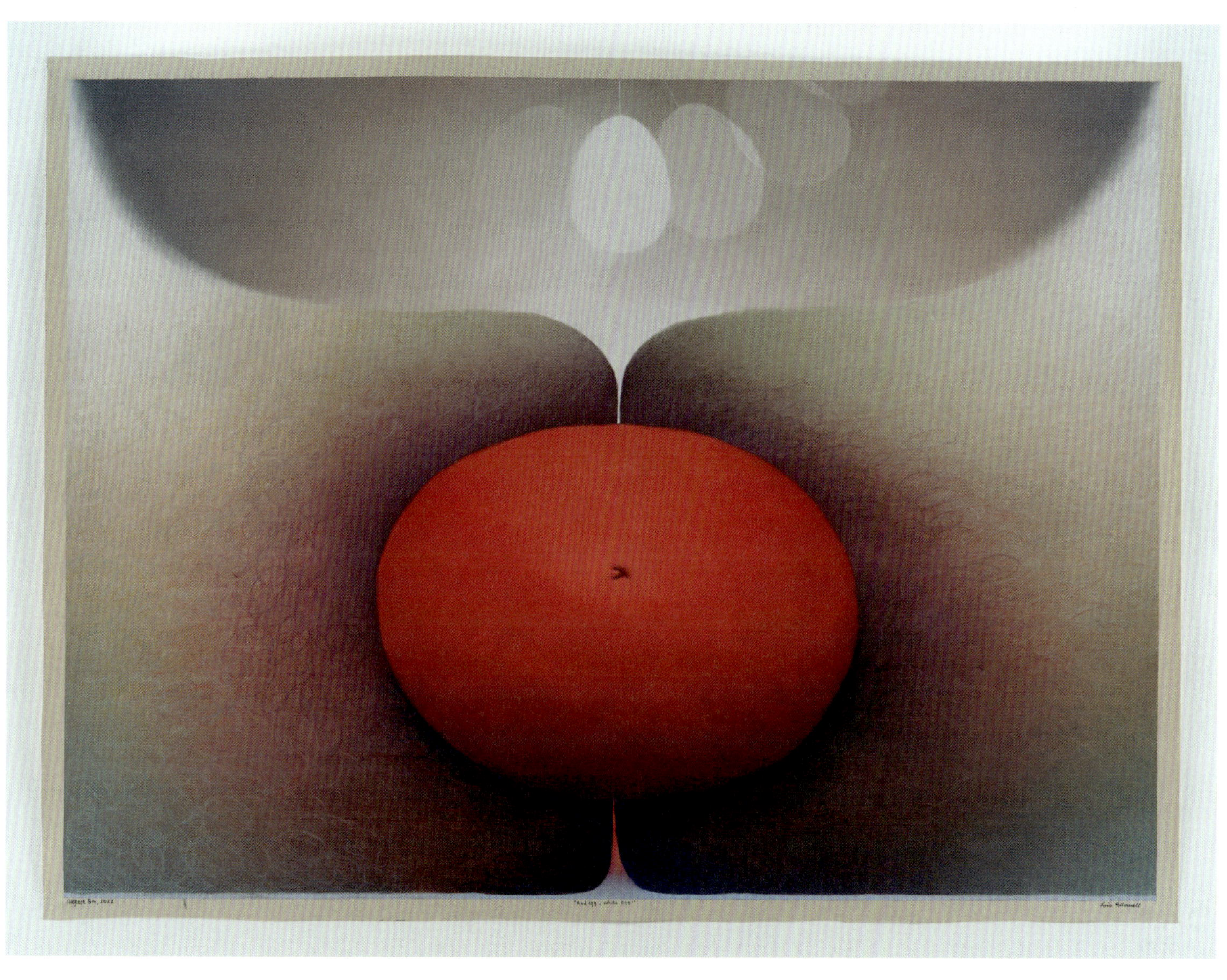

44.
Red egg, white egg
August 8, 2022

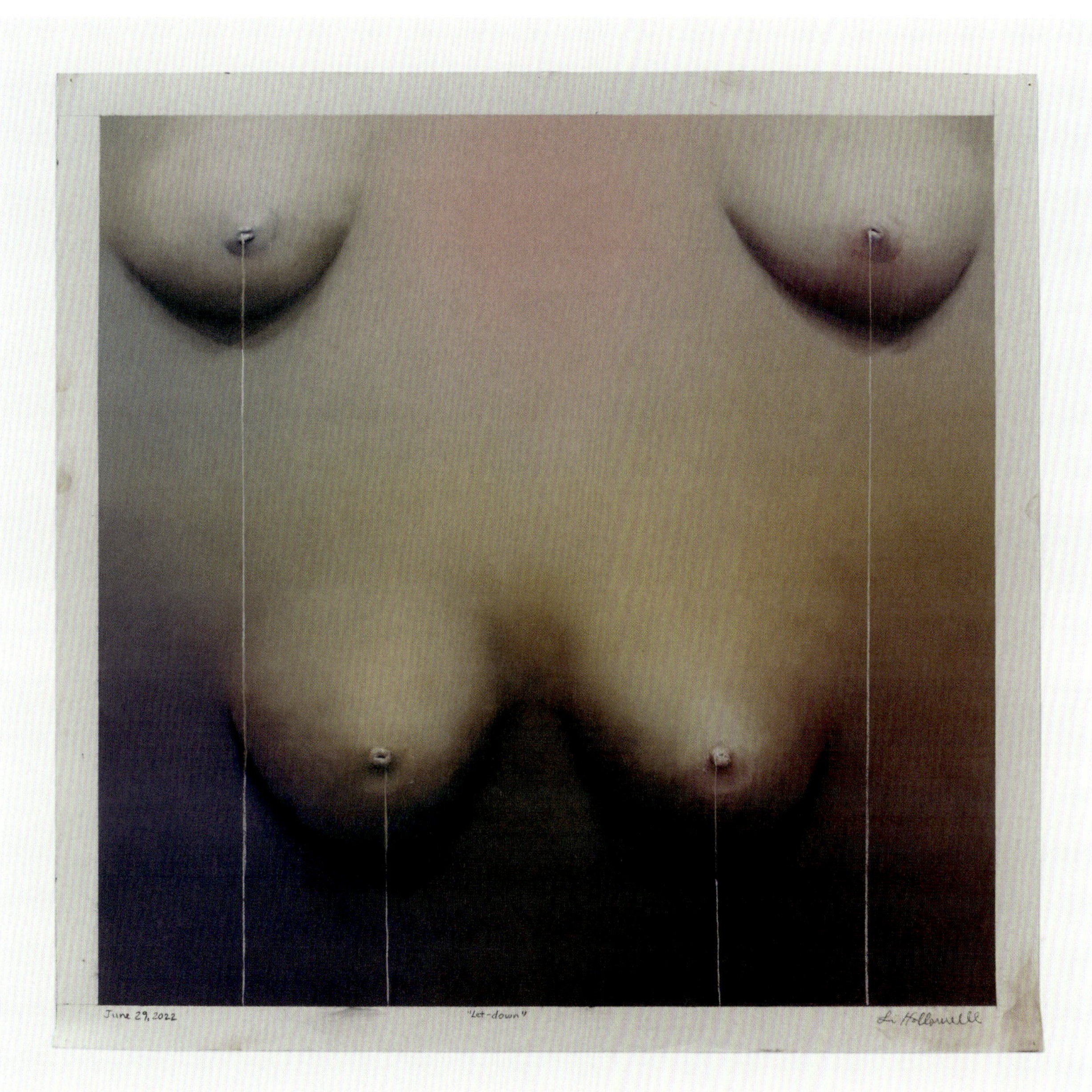

39.
Let-down
June 29, 2022

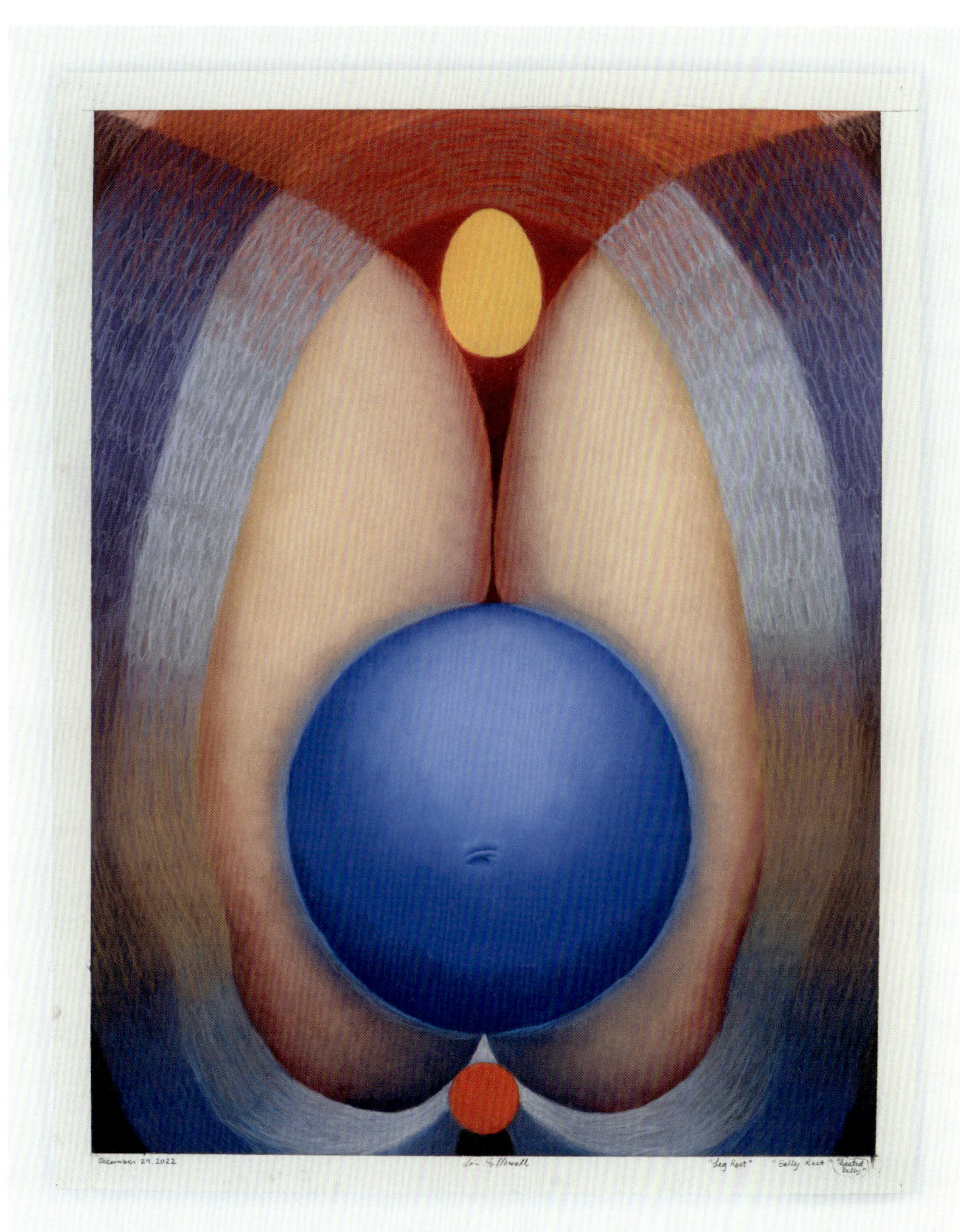

40.
Seated Belly
December 29, 2022

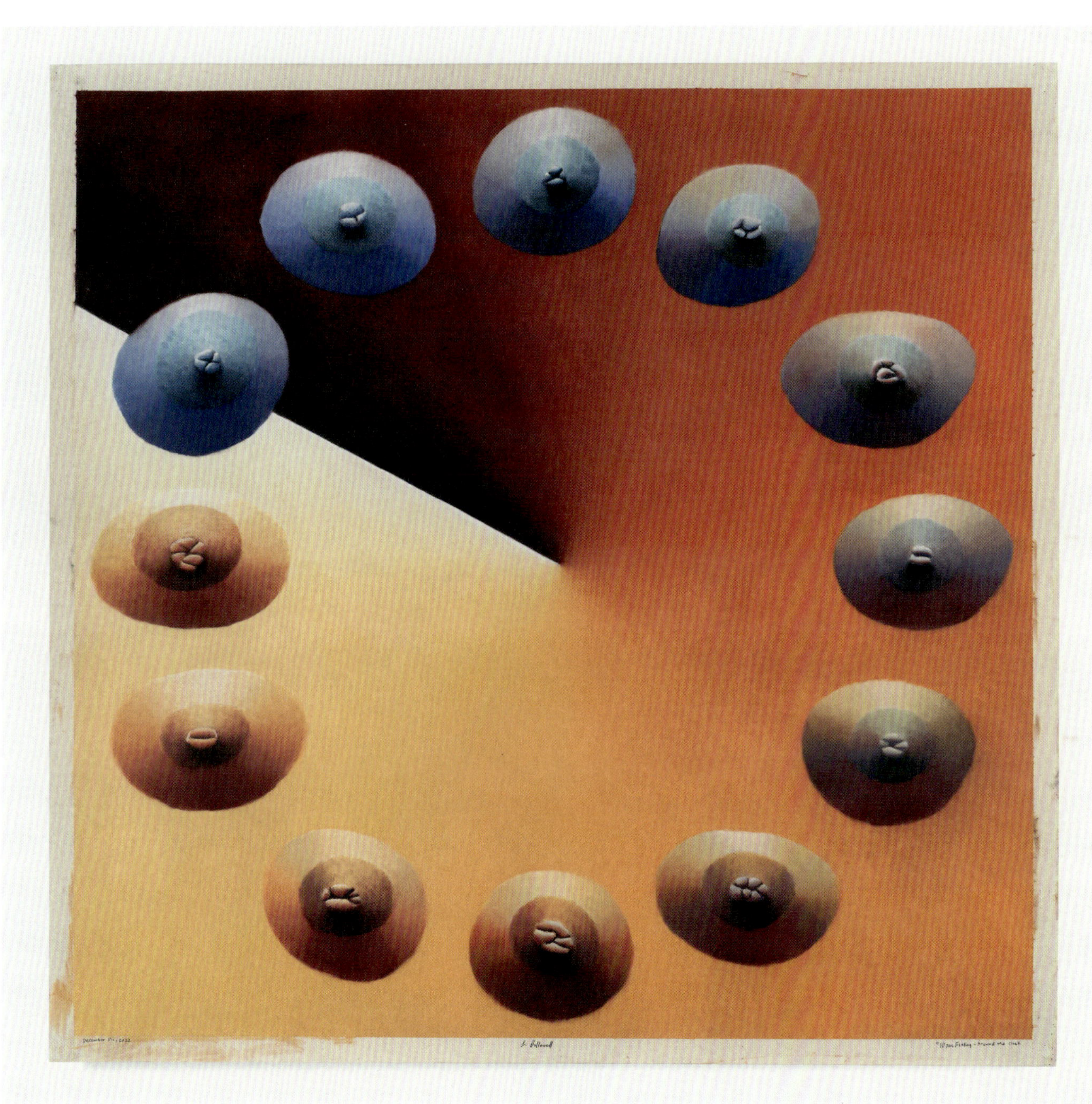

41.
10pm Feeding - Around the clock
December 5, 2022

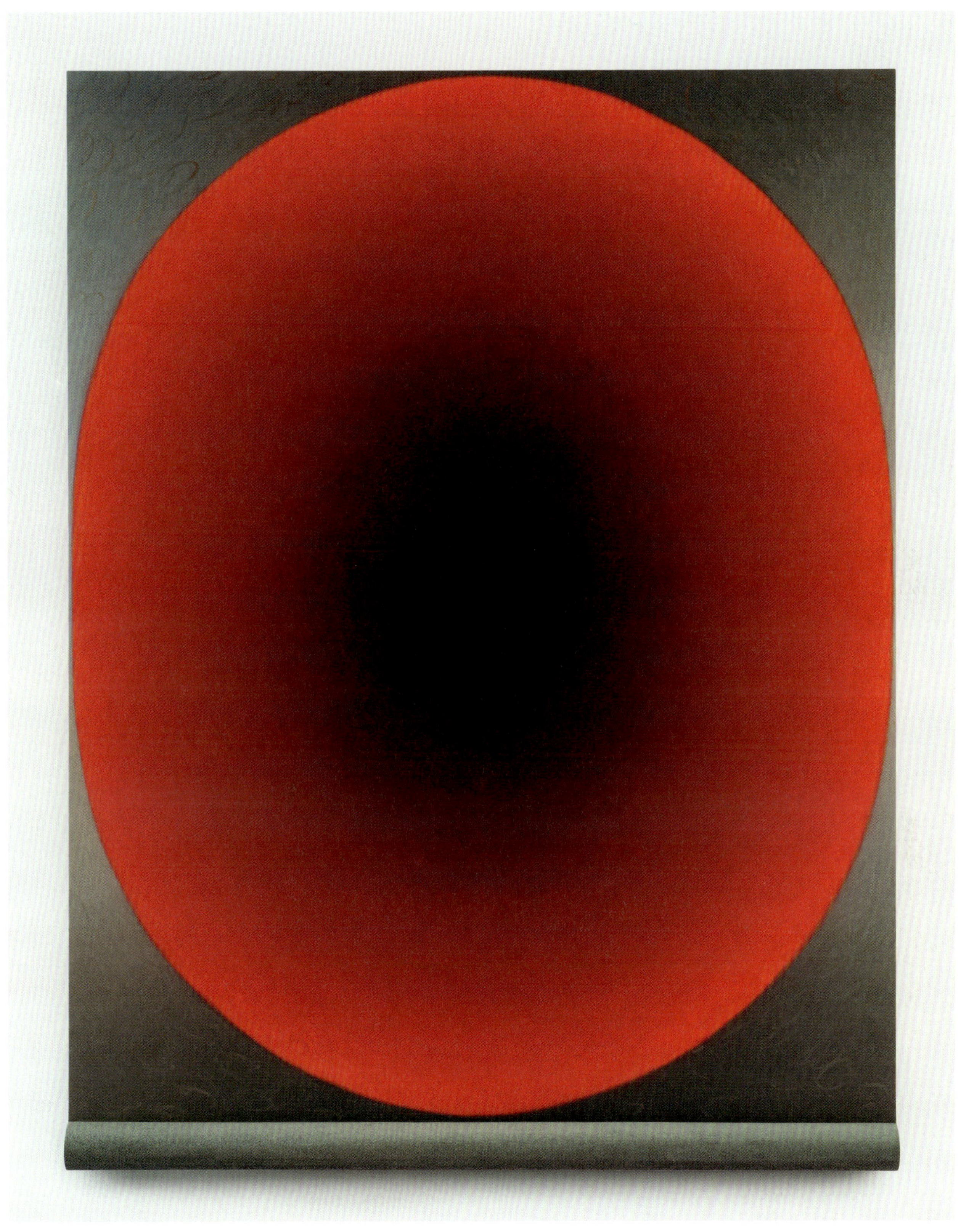

42.
Scarlet Brain, 2022

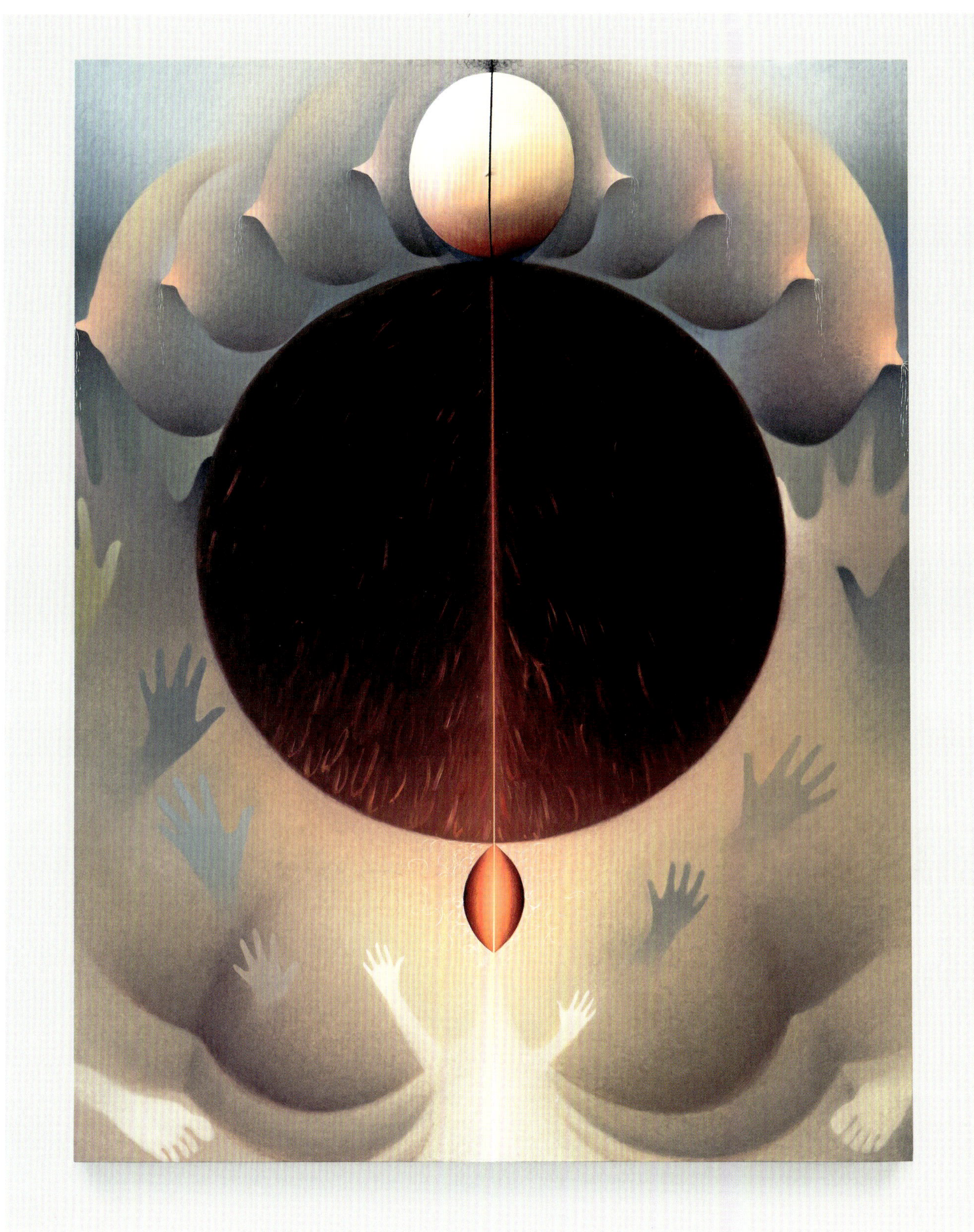

43.
Empty Belly, 2021

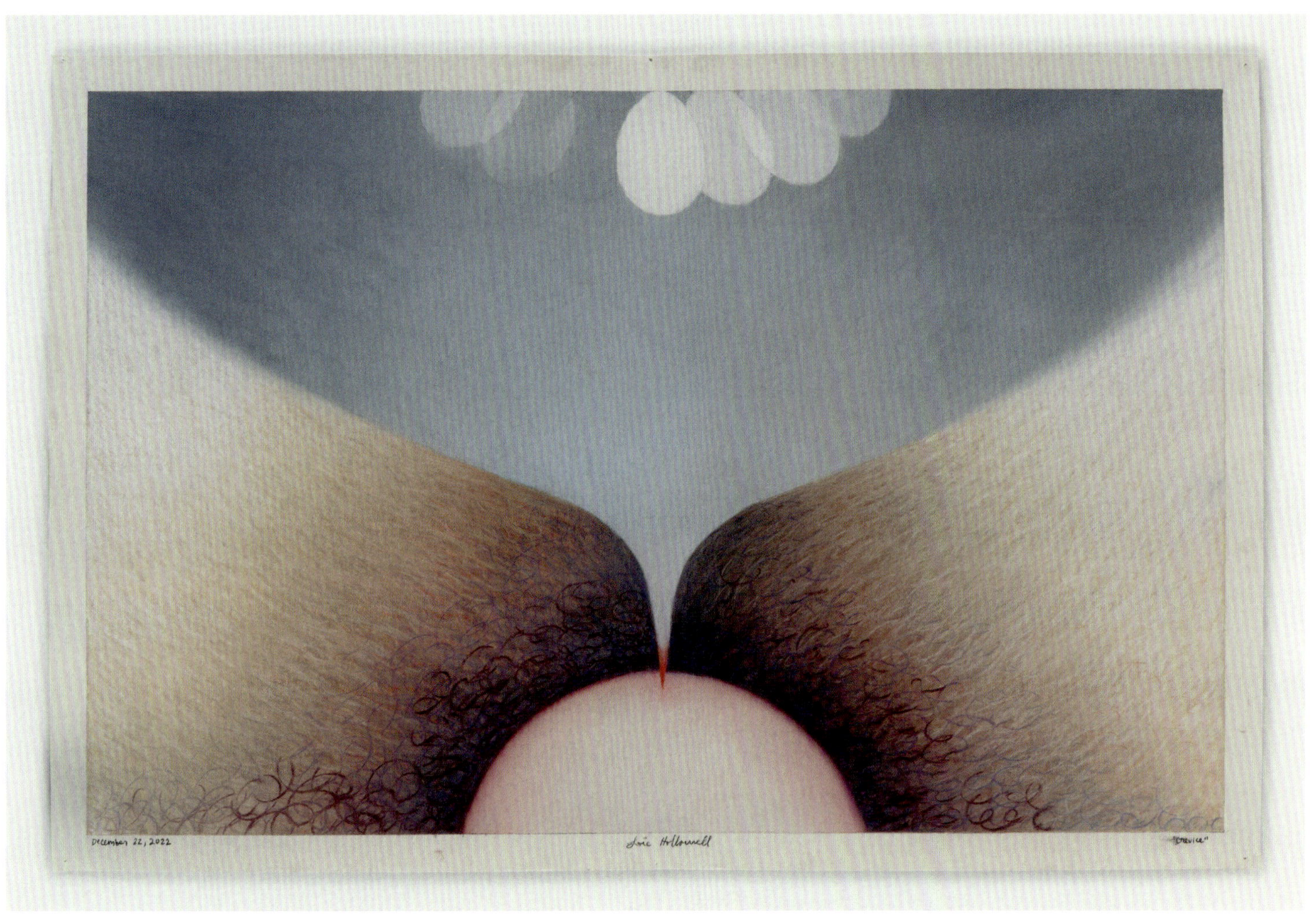

45.
Crevice
December 22, 2022

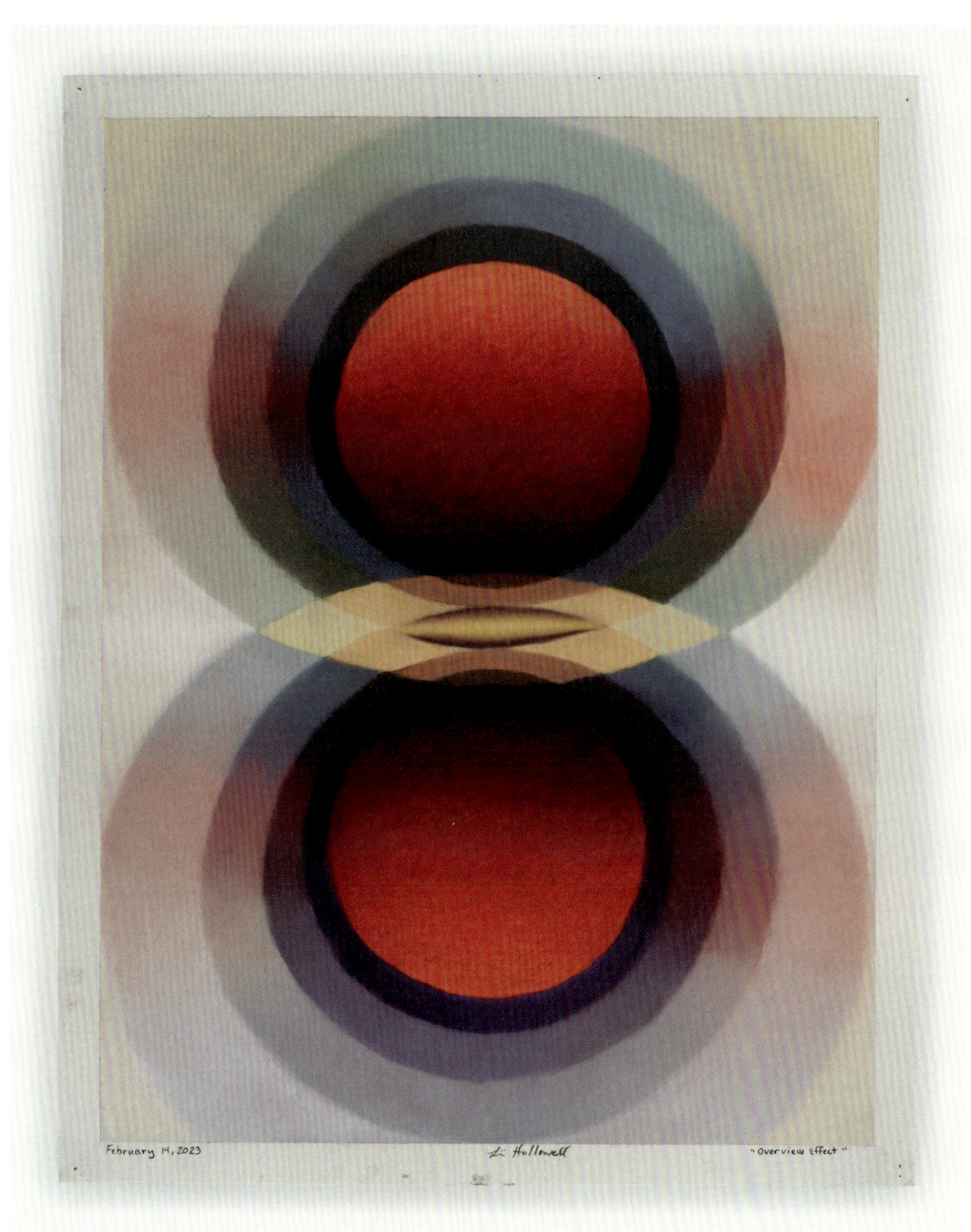

46.
Overview Effect
February 14, 2023

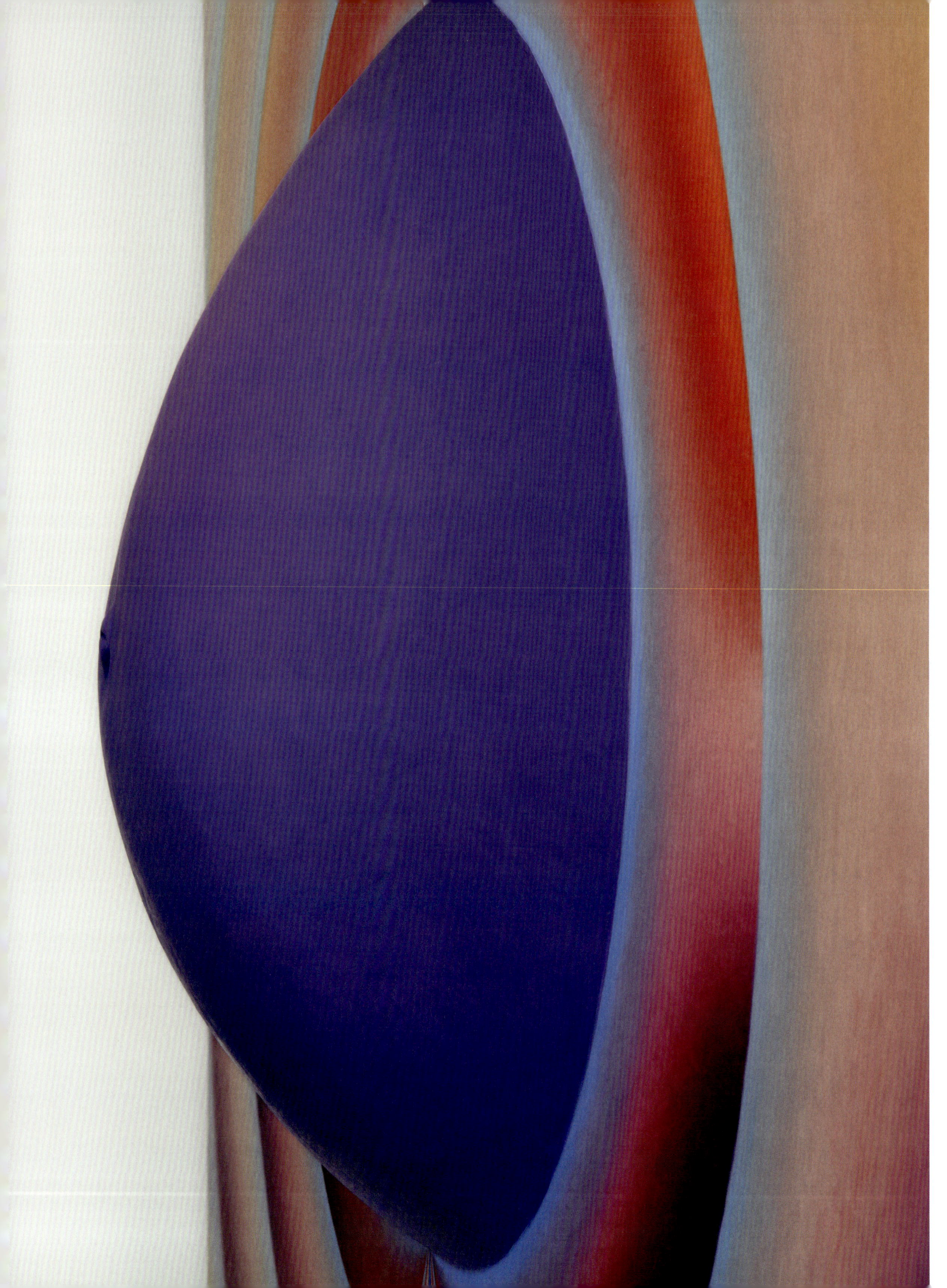

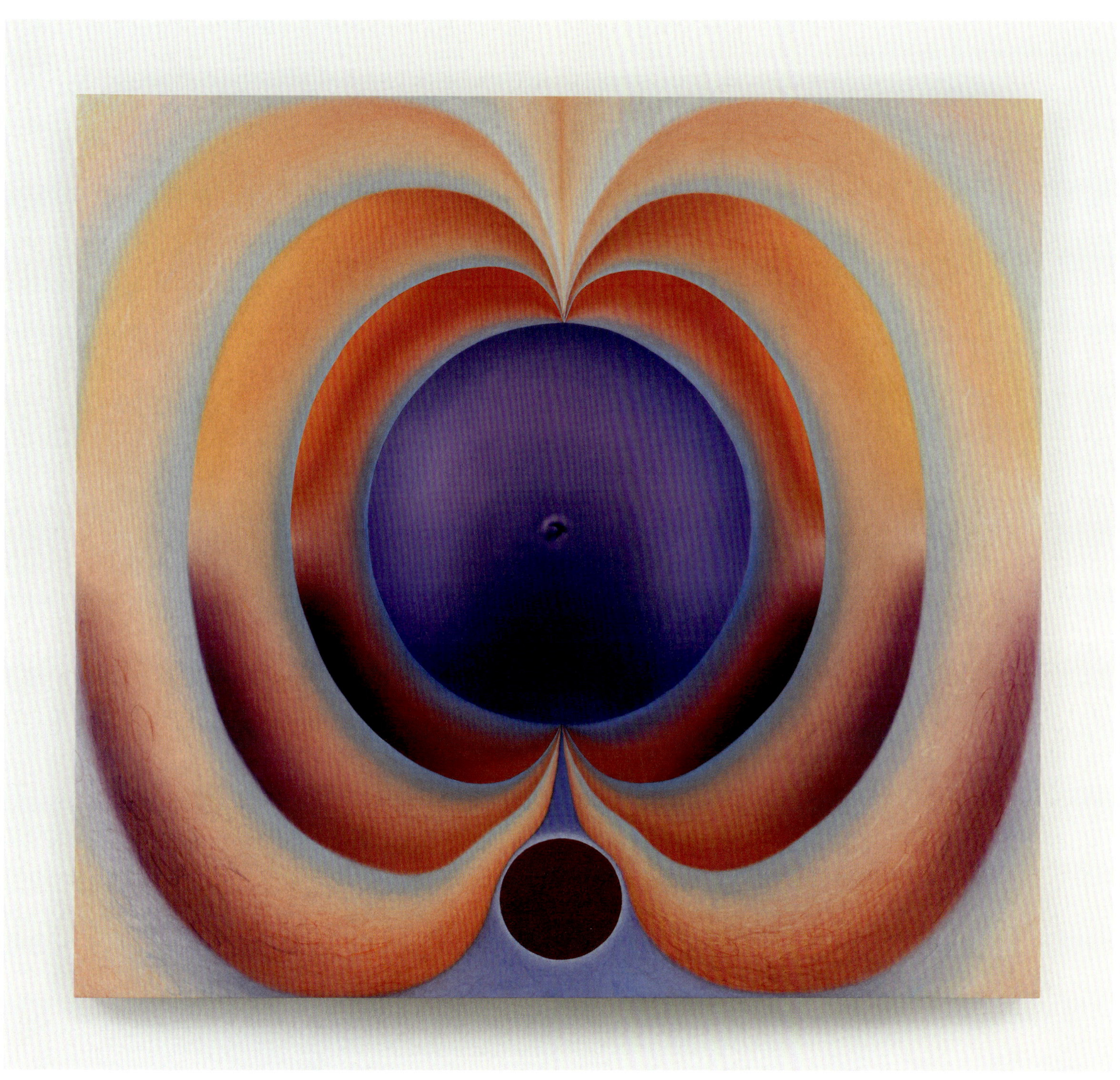

47.
Eight Centimeters Dilated in purple, blue, red and yellow, 2023

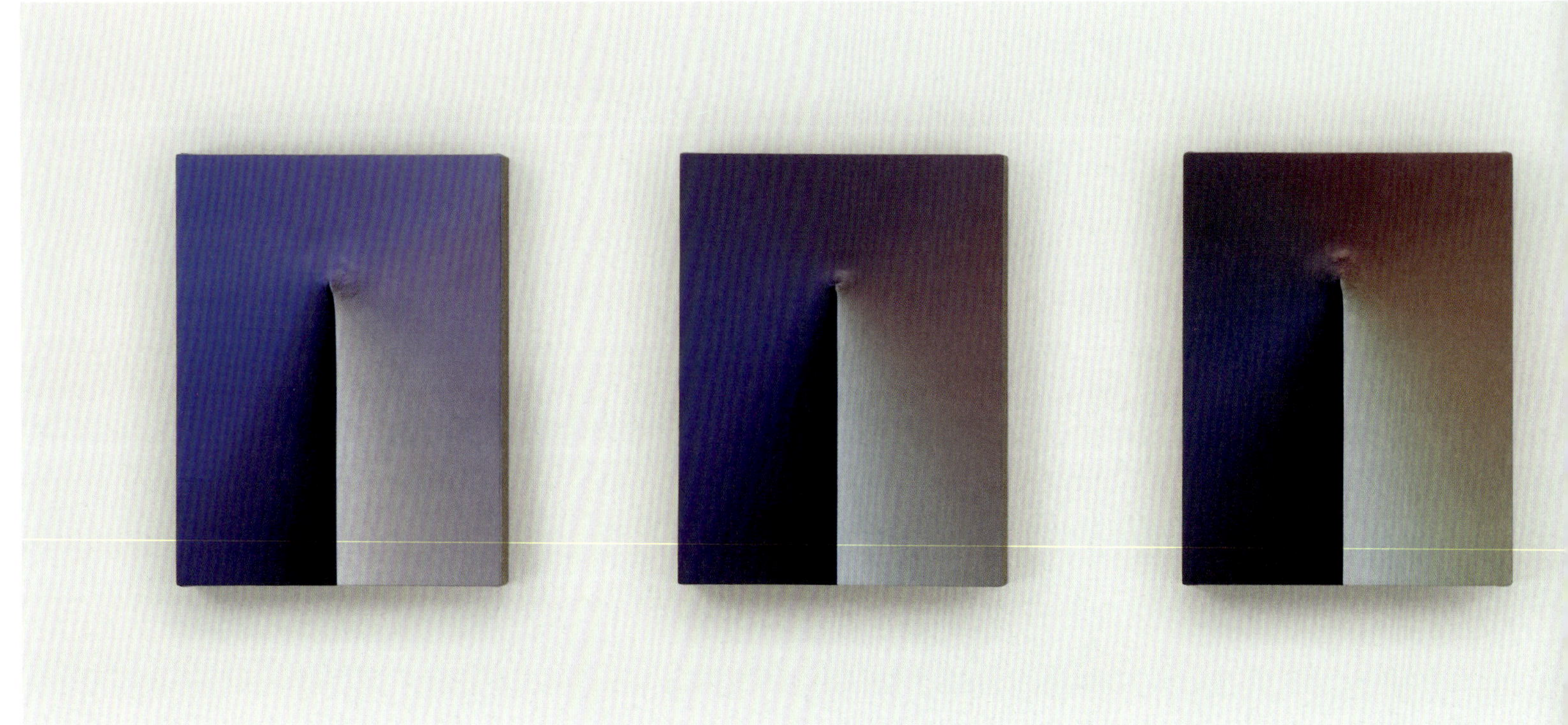

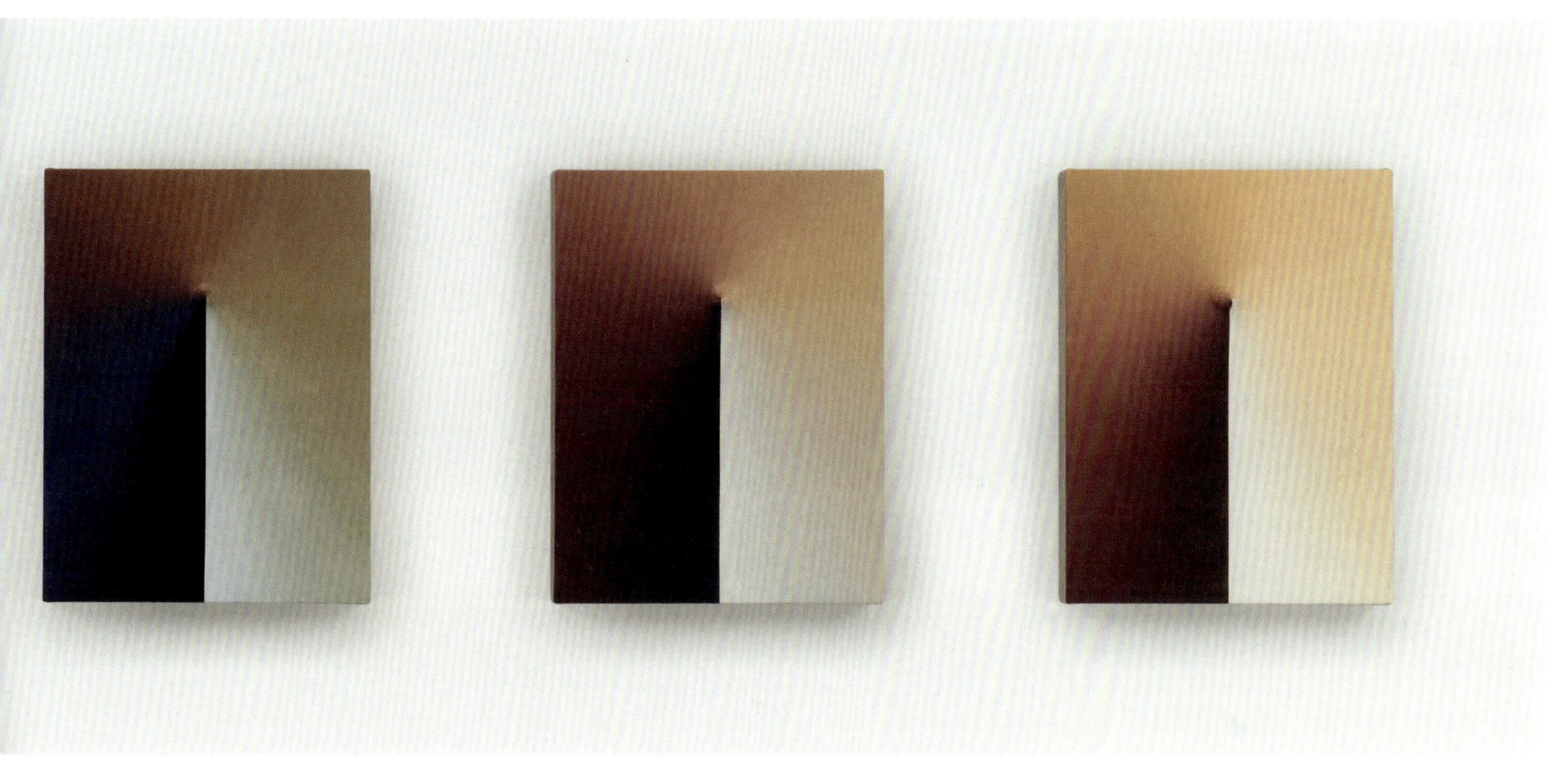

48.
11pm, 1am, 3am, 5am, 7am, 9am, 2023

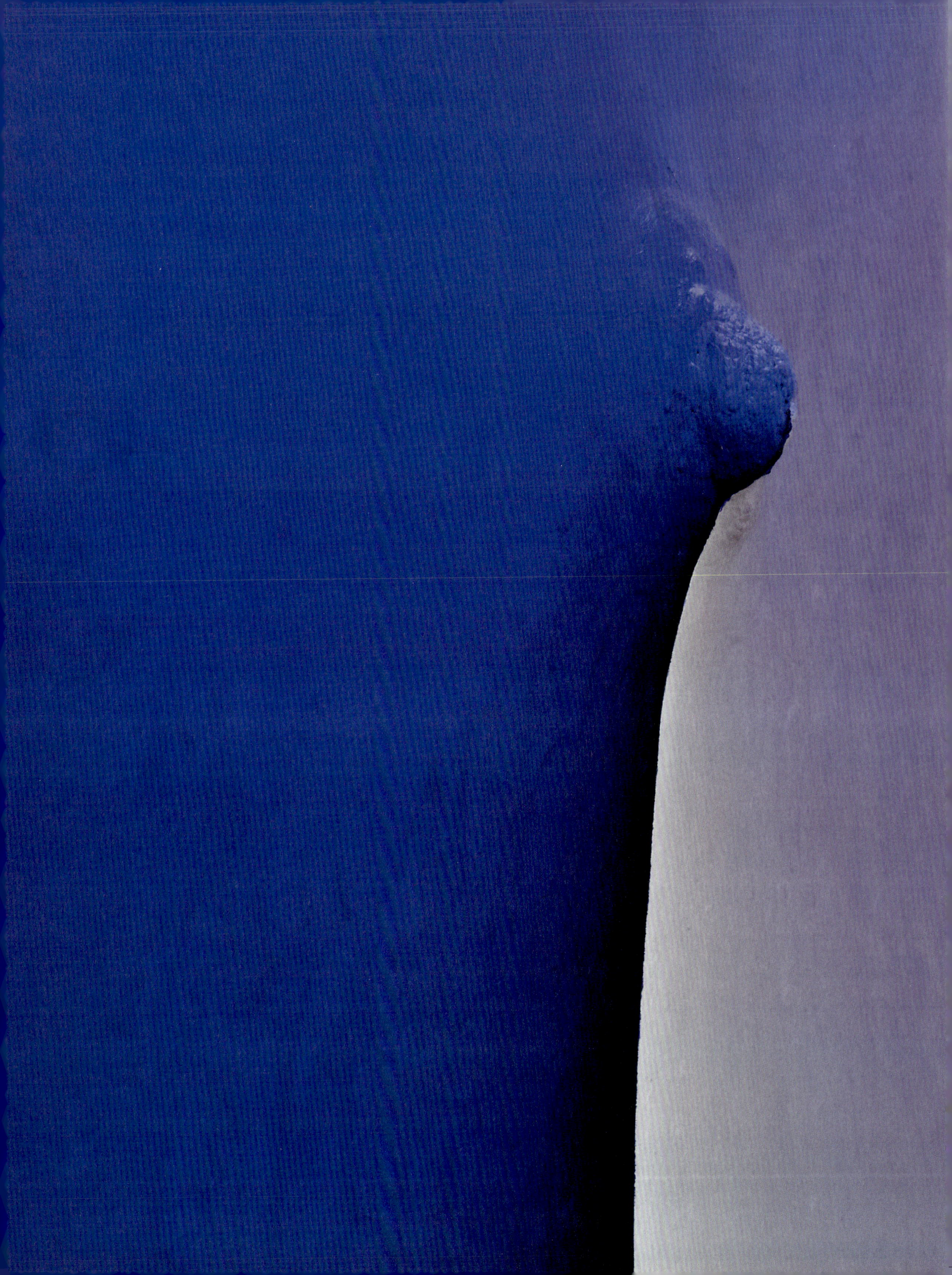

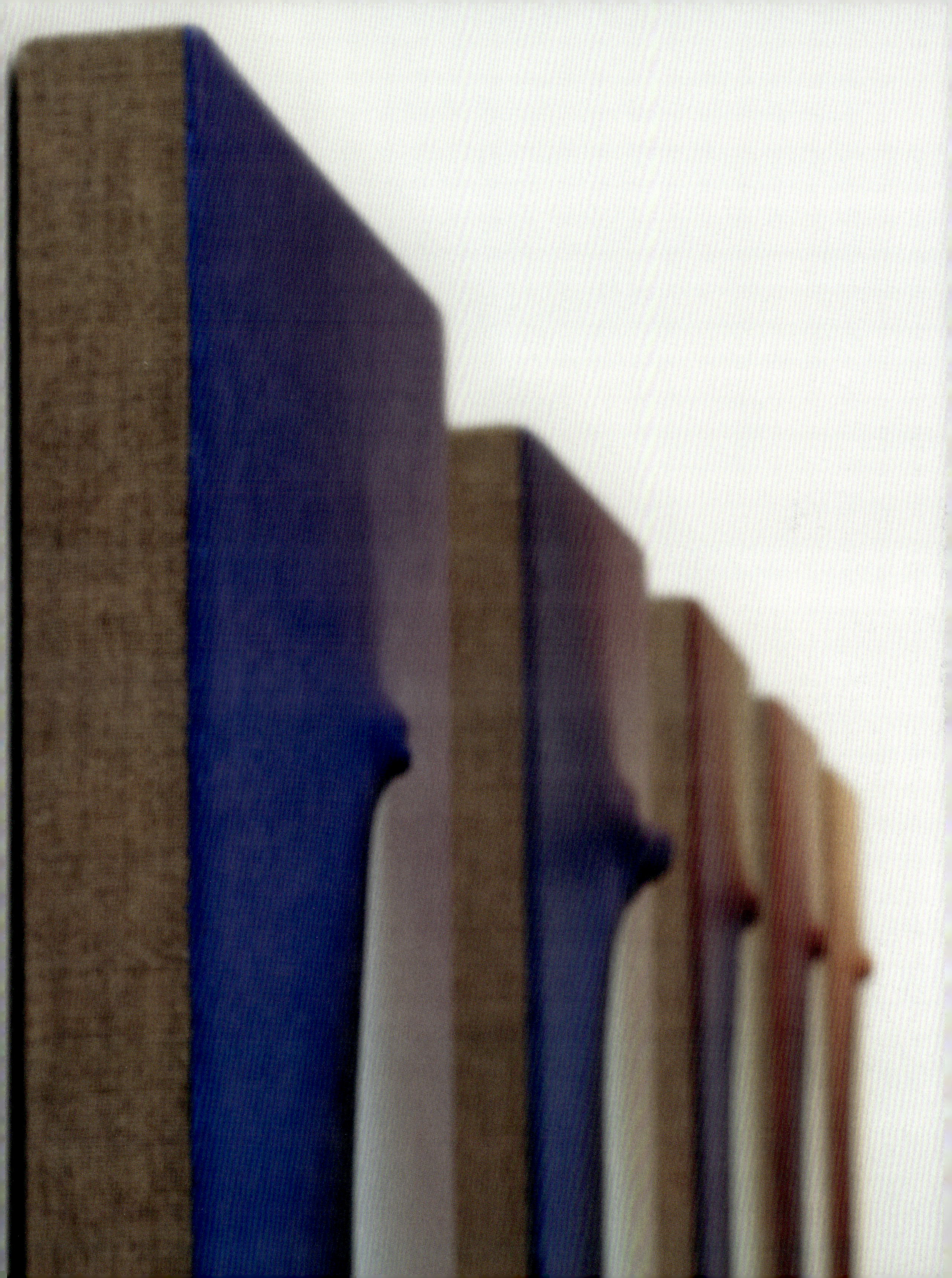

List of Works
All dimensions h x w x d in inches unless otherwise noted.

* Works included in the exhibition *Loie Hollowell: Space Between, A Survey of Ten Years*

*Happy Vagina**
October 20, 2013
Graphite on paper
12 x 9
Collection of the artist

*Emerald Mountain**
December 23, 2013
Charcoal and graphite on paper
12 x 9
Collection of the artist

*Diamond in reflection of sun on water**
September 2014
Soft pastel and graphite on paper
12 x 9
Collection of the artist

Circle, Oval, Hairy Mound, 2014
Oil on linen over panel
13 x 9
Private collection

Emerald Mountain, 2014
Oil on linen over panel
13 x 9
Private collection

Subterranean Eruption, 2014
Oil on linen over panel
13 x 9
Private collection

V, 2014
Oil on linen over panel
13 x 9
Private collection

*Giving Head**
February 3, 2015
Soft pastel and graphite on paper
12 x 9
Collection of the artist

*Peak**
June 13, 2015
Soft pastel and graphite on paper
12 x 9
Collection of the artist

*Portrait of a woman with green hair**
June 15, 2015
Soft pastel and graphite on paper
12 x 9
Collection of the artist

*Lick Lick (Red & Blue & Yellow)**
August 2015
Soft pastel on paper
12 x 9
Collection of the artist

Concentric Vibes in Orange and Blue, 2015
Oil on linen over panel
28 x 21
Private collection

Fire Line, 2015
Oil on linen over panel
28 x 21
Private collection

Linked Lingams in Green, Purple and Red, 2015
Oil on linen over panel
28 x 21
Private collection

*Bouncing on the Bed**
February 2016
Soft pastel and graphite on paper
12 x 9
Collection of the artist

*Pushed out by dicks**
February 2016
Soft pastel and graphite on paper
12 x 9
Collection of the artist

*Mountainscape**
April 11, 2016
Soft pastel and graphite on paper
12 x 9
Collection of the artist

*Boob Wheel**
June 12, 2016
Soft pastel and graphite on paper
12 x 9
Collection of the artist

*The Let Down**
June 13, 2016
Soft pastel and graphite on paper
12 x 9
Collection of the artist

Body of Water (in Yellow), 2016*
Oil, acrylic medium, sawdust, and high-density foam on linen over panel
48 x 36 x 2½
Private collection

Full Frontal (in Green), 2016
Oil, acrylic medium, sawdust, and high-density foam on linen over panel
48 x 36
Private collection

Stacked Lingam in red, yellow, purple and green, 2016*
Oil, acrylic medium, sawdust, and high-density foam on linen over panel
48 x 36 x 2¼
Private collection

Yellow Mountains, 2016*
Oil, acrylic medium, sawdust, and high-density foam on linen over panel
48 x 36 x 3
Collection of the artist

*Space Between (from one end to the other)**
April 9, 2017
Soft pastel and graphite on paper
16 x 12
Collection of the artist

*Point of Entry (orange moon over yellow sac)**
July 17, 2017
Soft pastel and graphite on paper
16 x 12
Collection of the artist

*Meeting at the Tip**
October 2, 2017
Soft pastel and graphite on paper
16 x 12
Collection of the artist

Point of Entry (blue green mounds over yellow sky), 2017*
Oil, acrylic medium, sawdust, and high-density foam on linen over panel
48 x 36 x 2½
Courtesy of Carolina Zapf & John Josephson

Point of Entry (lingam between red circles), 2017*
Oil, acrylic medium, sawdust, and high-density foam on linen over panel
48 x 36 x 3½
Private collection

The Lands Part (blue, red and purple), 2017*
Oil, acrylic medium, sawdust, and high-density foam on linen over panel
48 x 36 x 3½
The Collection of Dr. Robert Westerholm and Monica Wesley

*Egg Drop**
February 2018
Soft pastel and graphite on paper
16 x 12
Collection of the artist

*Balancing the scale**
October 30, 2018
Soft pastel and graphite on paper
16 x 12
Collection of the artist

*Into the depths**
January 7, 2019
Soft pastel and graphite on paper
16 x 12
Collection of the artist

*Red Slip**
February 14, 2019
Soft pastel and graphite on paper
16 x 12
Collection of the artist

Prenatal Plumb Line, 2019*
Oil, acrylic medium, and high-density foam on linen over panel
72 x 54 x 3½
Private collection

Red Hole, 2019*
Oil, acrylic medium, and high-density foam on linen over panel
72⅛ x 54 x 3¼
Private collection

Standing in yellow, pink and blue, 2019*
Oil, acrylic medium, and high-density foam on linen over panel
72 x 54 x 3¾
Collection of the artist

Empty Belly, 2021
Oil, acrylic medium, aqua resin, and epoxy resin on linen over panel
72 x 54 x 6
Private collection

Split Orbs in teal and mauve, 2021*
Oil, acrylic medium, and high-density foam on linen over panel
48 x 36 x 3¾
Private collection, CT

Tick-Tock Belly Clock, 2021*
Oil, acrylic medium, and epoxy resin on linen over panel
21 x 21 x 5
Collection of the artist

*Let-down**
June 29, 2022
Soft pastel on paper
23¼ x 23¼
Collection of the artist

*Red egg, white egg**
August 8, 2022
Soft pastel on paper
39½ x 52½
Courtesy of the artist and Pace Gallery

*10pm Feeding - Around the clock**
December 5, 2022
Soft pastel on paper
48½ x 48½
Collection of the artist

*Crevice**
December 22, 2022
Soft pastel on paper
26 x 38
Courtesy of the artist and Pace Gallery

*Seated Belly**
December 29, 2022
Soft pastel on paper
30 x 23
Courtesy of the artist and Pace Gallery

Scarlet Brain, 2022*
Oil, acrylic medium, and high-density foam on linen over Dibond and wood panel
72 x 54 x 3½
Collection of the artist

*Overview Effect**
February 14, 2023
Soft pastel on paper
25 x 20
Collection of the artist

11pm, 1am, 3am, 5am, 7am, 9am, 2023*
Oil, acrylic medium, aqua resin, epoxy resin, and sawdust on linen over panel
12 x 9 x 2½ (each)
Collection of the artist

Eight Centimeters Dilated in purple, blue, red and yellow, 2023*
Oil, acrylic medium, aqua resin, and epoxy resin on linen over panel
45 x 48
Courtesy of the artist and Pace Gallery

Staff

Eduardo Andres Alfonso
Associate Curator

Katie Bassett Langin
Registrar

Namulen Bayarsaihan
Director of Education

Cailin Briggs
Development Assistant

Maria Damato
Education Manager

Emily Devoe
Director of Marketing and Communications

Karen Gallego
Visitor Experience Manager

Susie Hamilton
Accountant

Holly Hart
Head of Membership and Events

Kris Honeycutt
Director of Development

Brian Kibler
Head of Installation and Facilities

Gretchen Kraus
Design Director

Holly Lapine
Education and Access Specialist

Gina Mello
Director of Finance and Administration

Caitlin Monachino
Curatorial and Publications Manager

Antonio Paone
Education Assistant

Gloria Perez
Digital Media and Marketing Coordinator

Amy Smith-Stewart
Chief Curator

Barbara Toplin
Volunteer Archivist

Photography Credits

FIG. 1
Frida Kahlo
Henry Ford Hospital, 1932
Oil on metal
12 x 15 in.
Museo Dolores Olmedo Patiño/Mexico City, DF/ Mexico
© 2024 Banco de México Diego Rivera Frida Kahlo Museums Trust, Mexico, D.F. / Artists Rights Society (ARS), New York

FIG. 2
Louise Bourgeois
UNTITLED (WOMAN GIVING BIRTH), 1941
Ink and pencil on graph paper
11 x 8½ in.
Collection Kunstmuseum Bern, Switzerland
Photo: Eeva Inkeri
© The Easton Foundation/ Licensed by VAGA at Artists Rights Society (ARS), NY

FIG. 3
Clarity Haynes
Blood Altar, 2023
Oil on canvas
63 x 64 in.
Courtesy of the artist and New Discretions

FIG. 4
Luchita Hurtado
Untitled (Birthing Mother Earth), 2018
Acrylic and ink on linen
24 x 19 x 1⅝ in.
© The Estate of Luchita Hurtado
Courtesy The Estate of Luchita Hurtado and Hauser & Wirth
Photo: Jeff McLane

FIG. 5
Ithell Colquhoun
Scylla, 1938
Oil paint on board
36 x 24 in. (support)
40 x 28 x 3 in. (frame)
Tate, purchased 1977
© Samaritans, © Noise Abatement Society & © Spire Healthcare
Photo: © Tate

FIG. 6
Suellen Rocca
Ring Girl, c. 1965
Oil on canvas
84¼ x 60 in.
Minneapolis Institute of Art, Gift of Dennis Adrian in honor of the artist, 2017.21.2

Courtesy Matthew Marks Gallery
Photo: Minneapolis Institute of Art

FIG. 7
Hannah Wilke
Untitled, 1979
Chewing gum sculpture in Plexiglas box
2½ x 2½ x 1 in.
Hannah Wilke Collection & Archive, Los Angeles

Courtesy Alison Jacques, London
Photo: Michael Brzinszki

FIG. 8
Emil James Bisttram
The Flaming One, 1964
Oil on canvas
48 x 34 in.
Promised gift to the New Mexico Museum of Art from William Dailey and Nicole Panter Dailey

FIG. 9
Ana Mendieta
Untitled: Silueta Series, Iowa, 1976–78

Courtesy Galerie Lelong & Co.
Licensed by Artists Rights Society (ARS), New York

FIG. 10
Zilia Sánchez
Las Amazonas [The Amazons], 1968
Acrylic on stretched canvas
72 x 108 x 13½ in.
Lent by the Tate Americas Foundation, purchased using endowment income and courtesy of the Latin American Acquisitions Committee 2019

Courtesy Galerie Lelong & Co., New York
Photo: © Tate

FIG. 11
Harmony Hammond
Green, 1976
Oil and Dorland's Wax Medium on canvas
15 x 60 in.

Courtesy of the artist and Alexander Gray Associates, New York
Photo: John Vokoun

FIG. 12
Helen Pashgian
Untitled, 2020
Cast epoxy with formed acrylic elements
6 in. (sphere diameter)
54½ x 3 x 3 in. (pedestal)
60½ x 6 x 6 in. (overall)

Courtesy the artist and Lehmann Maupin, New York, Seoul, and London
Photo: Daniel Kukla

FIG. 13
G.R. Santosh
Shakti vichor, 1982

FIG. 14
Anonymous, Untitled, 2000, Sanganer & Delhi from *Tantra Song: Tantric Painting from Rajasthan*, edited by Franck André Jamme, Siglio, 2011

FIG. 15
Attributed to the Schuster Master (Cycladic, active about 2400 B.C.)
Female Figure of the Late Spedos Type, about 2400 B.C.
Marble
16 x 5³⁄₁₆ x 1 1⁵⁄₁₆ in.
The J. Paul Getty Museum, Villa Collection, Malibu, California, 90.AA.114
Digital image courtesy of Getty's Open Content Program

*All plates mentioned below include the detail images of the work unless otherwise mentioned.

Feuer/Mesler, New York:
Plates 5, 8, 11
Gloria Perez:
Plate 9 detail, plate 11 detail
Jason Mandella:
Page 6, plate 43
JSP Art Photography:
Plates 6, 7
Kerry Ryan McFate, Courtesy Pace Gallery:
Plates 9, 14
Loie Hollowell:
Plates 1–4
Melissa Goodwin, Courtesy Pace Gallery:
Plates 10, 13, 15, 16, 19, 20, 23, 31—34, 38, 40, 42, 44–48
Melissa Goodwin & Robyn Caspare, Courtesy Pace Gallery:
Plates 17, 18, 39, 41
Rich Lee, Courtesy Pace Gallery:
Plates 21, 22, 24—30, 35—37
Tom Barratt, Courtesy Pace Gallery:
Plate 12

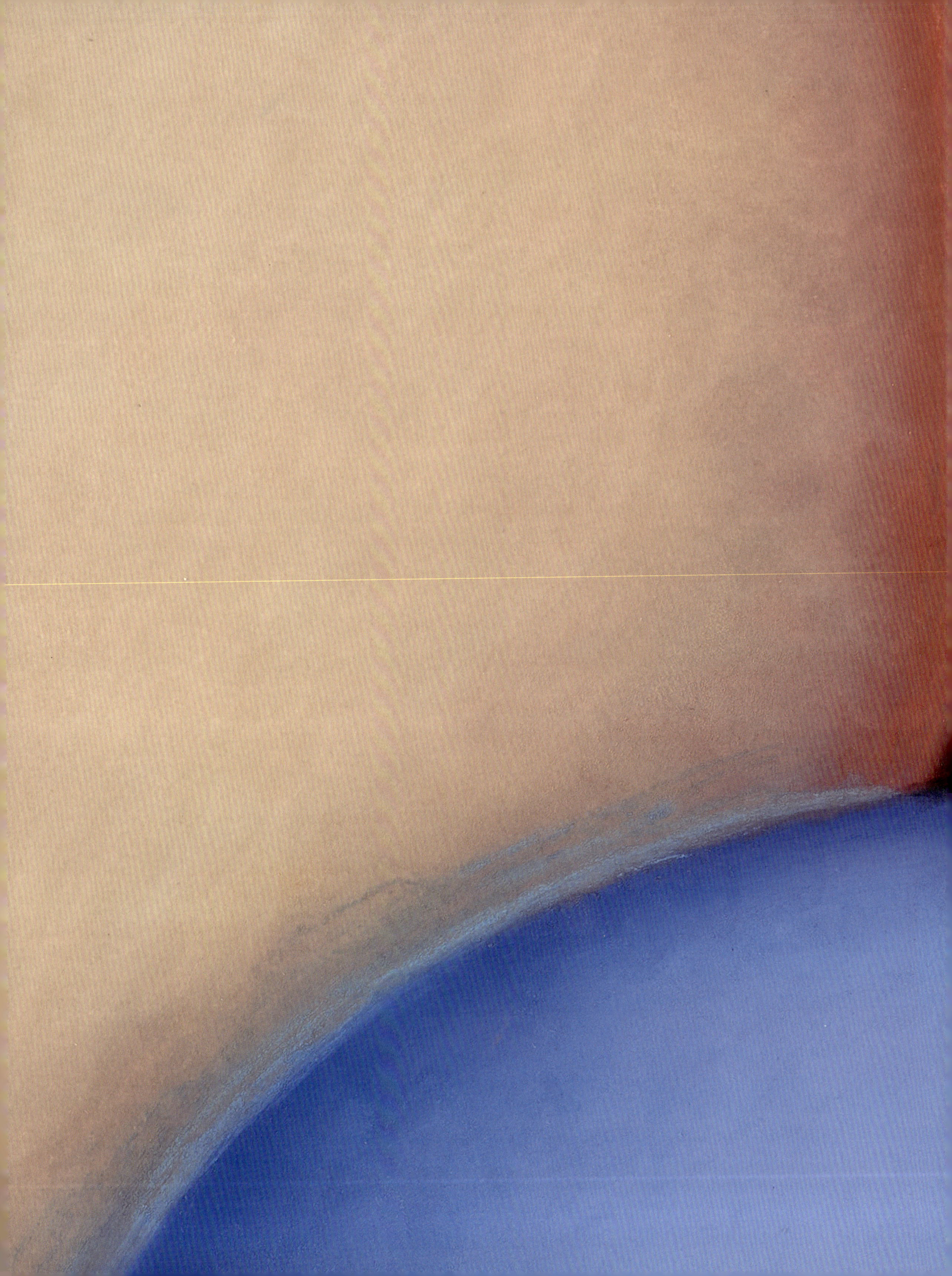

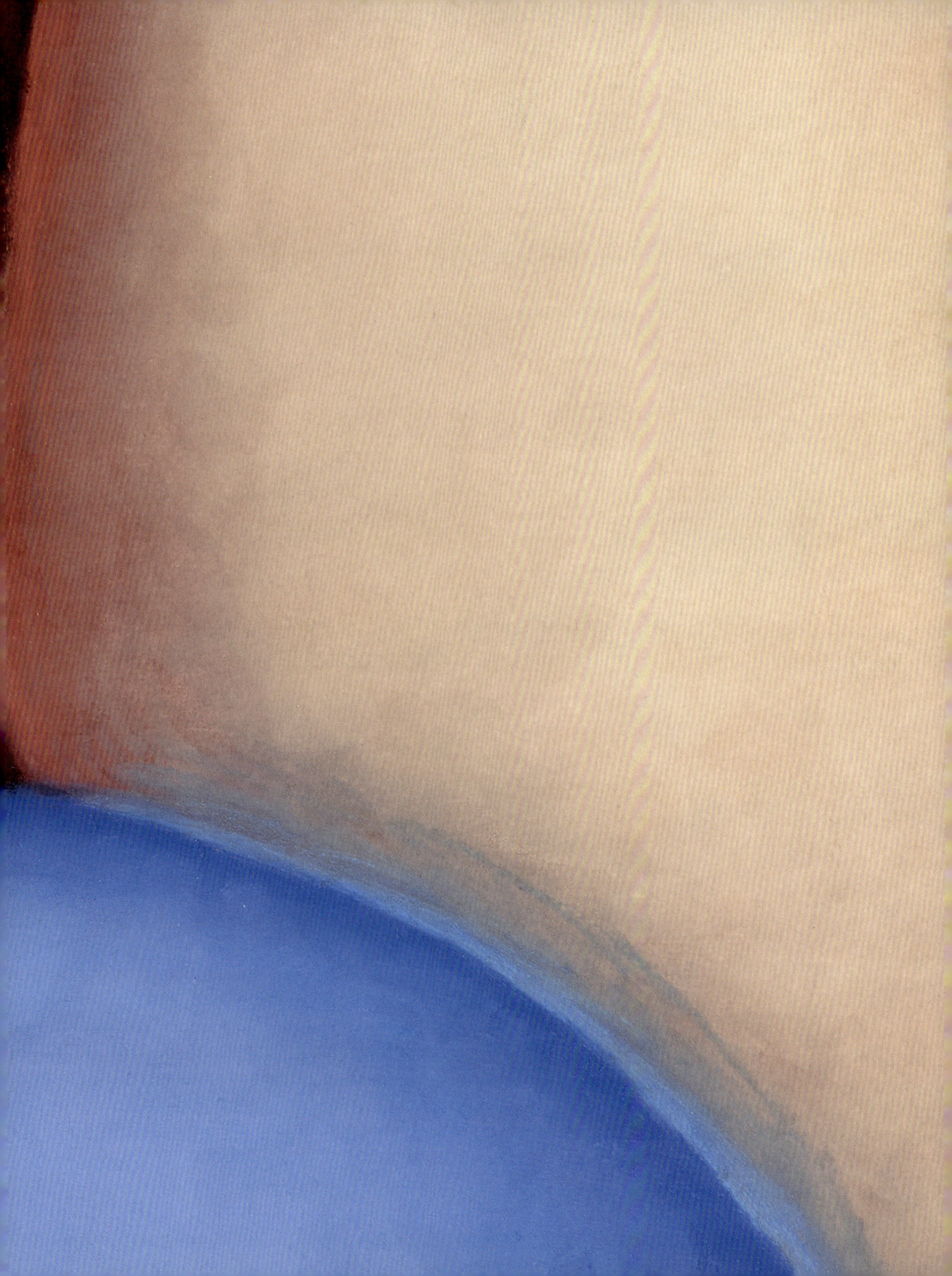

Published on the occasion of the exhibition *Loie Hollowell: Space Between, A Survey of Ten Years,* organized by The Aldrich Contemporary Art Museum, January 21 to August 11, 2024

Institute for Contemporary Art at Virginia Commonwealth University
September 6, 2024 to March 9, 2025

Loie Hollowell: Space Between, A Survey of Ten Years is curated by Amy Smith-Stewart, Chief Curator.

Catalogue Design:
Gretchen Kraus
Production Manager:
Caitlin Monachino
Copy Editors:
Mary Cason and
Katie Brennan
Printer: Conti Tipocolor, Florence, Italy

PP. 2–3, 88–89, cover:
Seated Belly
December 29, 2022
Courtesy of the artist and Pace Gallery
Photo: Melissa Goodwin, Courtesy Pace Gallery

The Aldrich Contemporary Art Museum

The Aldrich
Contemporary Art
Museum
258 Main Street
Ridgefield, CT 06877
thealdrich.org

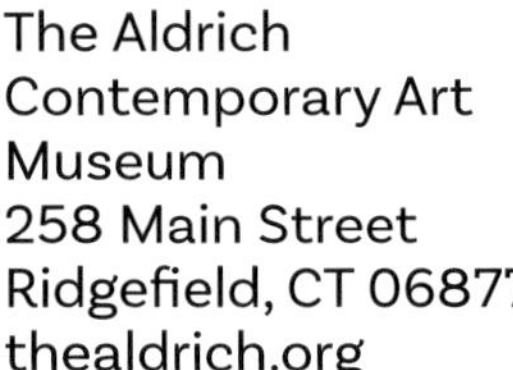

GREGORY R. MILLER & CO.

Gregory R. Miller & Co.
62 Cooper Square
New York, NY 10003
grmandco.com

Distributed worldwide by ARTBOOK | D.A.P.
artbook.com

ISBN: 9781941366721

Library of Congress Control Number: 2024940789

Generous support for *Loie Hollowell: Space Between, A Survey of Ten Years* is provided by Fairfax Dorn and Marc Glimcher and Jessica Silverman, San Francisco. Significant support is provided by Georganne Aldrich Heller; Tammy and Jay Levine; and James Park, San Francisco. The catalogue is supported by the Eric Diefenbach and James-Keith Brown Publications Fund, Girlfriend Fund, and Pace Gallery. Production support is provided by the Diana Bowes and Jim Torrey Commissions Fund.